Bismillah Khan

Bismillah Khan And Benaras

The Seat of Shehnai

BISMILLAH KHAN AND BENARAS

The Seat of Shehnai

By
Rita Ganguly

Foreword by
Raghava R. Menon

SIDDHI BOOKS
Imprint Of
COSMO PUBLICATIONS
1994
INDIA

ISBN 81-7020-679-0

Photo Credits: AVINASH PASRICHA
ZOOM STUDIO, BENARAS

Manufactured in India

Published by:
MRS. RANI KAPOOR
For SIDDHI BOOKS
Imprint of
COSMO PUBLICATIONS
FOR GENESIS PUBLISHING PVT. LTD.
24-B, Ansari Road, Darya Ganj,
New Delhi-110002. INDIA

Typeset by
Manav Computer House
Delhi-110092.

Printed at
ARUN & RAJIVE PVT. LTD.
New Delhi-110020, INDIA

Dedicated to:

SIDDHESHWARI DEVI

AND

BEGUM AKHTAR

Foreword

Rita Ganguly's account of the life and times of Ustad Bismillah Khan is a riveting account of, one of the most important musical spirits of this century in India.

Being a musician and a singer herself the author's approach to her subject is not that of a social scientist or a historian who comments and examines the historical and social perspectives of a human life. Her account is a musician's version of another musician's life. Its text has evidence of an insight and penetration rare in this kind of writing. The language is informal and carries the resonance of the spoken word, the impact of dialect which the music of the region of Benares exemplifies.

The Ustad is a spiritually awakened man and his life bears witness to a striking tranquility and repose which is the inner essence of an arrived human being. His art naturally portrays this inner quiet. A sound that is kindly compassionate and tolerant. The book has several nuggets of anecdotal material, and is rich in personal experience of the man and the impact he has had on the art of the *shehnai* which the *Ustad* brought to life in his time and bestowed upon his beloved country.

Having been a student of the two immortal *Divas* of Hindustani Music Siddheswari Devi and Begum Akhtar the personal authority of the author adds an important dimension to the book. I would like to wish this book to go forth and delight those who themselves have been entranced by the *shehnai* being written by one whose sensitive spirit fills its pages.

New Delhi,
Summer 1994.

Raghava R. Menon

Acknowledgement

My grateful thanks to Professor S.K. Saxena who inspired me to express whatever I felt, and gave me the insight to Indian Aesthetics.

Raghunath Prasanna, a great master of *shehnai* and flute and Mr. Massy of Varanasi, the eminent *tabla* player. A living legend Pt. Kishan Maharaj. To all other *shehnai* players who did not wish to co-operate.

And lastly Nupur Chakrabarty, without her help and hard-work, this work would not have been possible, as well as to Kothari family for bearing with my tantrums.

Contents

1

Rasa-The Basic Concept of Indian Aesthetics

INTRODUCTION

To appreciate and understand Ustad Bismillah Khan, it is very important to know the theory of Indian aesthetics. No amount of western methodology can amply compensate the understanding of *rasa* created by each individual artist in their realm of art. There is not one singular standard yard-stick. No one sweeping method or methodology that can help to comprehend the Indian performing art. As described by professor S.K. Saxena, it is the difference between salt and salty preparation, sugar and sweet cookies, bitter and a *subzi* of *karela*, pepper and a *chutney* preparation made of chilly and garlic sauce. Thus, as the Natyashashtra reveals, in India, performing art is presented like a *vyanjan*, a cooked dish. The name of the dish is invariably given after the main ingredient. So is it true with the sentiments—Love-*shringar*, valour-*veer*, anger-*roundra* and wonder-*adbhoot* which give birth to four more sentiments—sorrow-*karuna*, fear-*bhayanak*, disgust-*vibhatsa* and laughter-*hasya* respectively, and a ninth sentiment—peace. Each sentiment, under the heading of each of the other sentiments is used as ingredient. They are cooked in a vessel, and the vessel is the performer. Thus the performer is the *patra*. It is very simple to understand that if chicken curry is prepared, each ingredient, the chicken, onion, garlic, curd, chilly powder, cloves, oil, coconut, cardamom, and cinnamon seeds can not be eaten individually. Once they are cooked in correct proportions, it becomes curry. But the most important ingredient is the salt, where the individuality of the artist comes into play. All these ingredients cooked in proper temperature would make the curry, but if the curry is left in the bowl, it would mean nothing. The dish becomes significant only when it is tasted, and that tasting is done by the audience. This is called - *rasaswadan*. The raga or the sentiment that is cooked in the intellect of the artist with all the ingredients marvellously blent is presented to the audience. The ultimate award of the audience for tasting the cooked dish of the artist is the achievement of joy. Now, this theory has many detailed nuances discussed in the sixth chapter of the Natyashashtra. We are not going into the intricate descriptions; but the joy of tasting the cooked dish or the *rasaswadan* can be beautifully analyzed once you hear Ustad Bismillah Khan. You sway with his excellent rendering wondering all the time if it is the Benaras *ang*, or the Gwalior *gamak*, the *meend* of *Kirana gharana* or the purity of *raga* of the Agra *gharana*! It is difficult to put your finger in one singular element. You fail to understand what really enchants you, whether tonality or the tunefulness, the presentation of the party or the man, isolated from his party. You get enticed by his twinkling mischevious eyes which play tricks shining in the light of the stage. He seems to be enacting a romantic scene as a romantic hero, tickling and teasing the maiden with his immaculate *sur*, describing and flirting with his exquisite *layakari* and language of *raga*, and wooing the maiden with his impeccable technique. In brief that is how Ustad Bismillah Khan appears on the stage. It is an experience of total theatre.

An aspect of Indian aesthetics deals with *sadharanikaran* (making things ordinary), and *aloukik* (sublime). *Sadharanikaran*, is the explicit, sensous and worldly section of art or music which the artist or the musician presents to the audience or the people. It has a direct, tangible and overt influence over the mind, heart and soul of the people. It is an earthly impression, although the unearthly subtly weaves through. People who are interested in the *sadharanikaran*, the artist, musician, or the audience, get a touch of the supernatural, but others remain ignorant of the bliss. On the other hand, the *aloukik* part of the Indian aesthetics deals with the noble, refined and supersensible, which belongs to the realm of the unworldly, the spirit. Bismillah Khan's music pulls you above the mundane existence of tension, anxiety and ambition. The maestro creats a purely *aloukik*, sublime ambience for his listeners. He communes with the lightful world of the divine spirit, he communicates with his listeners with a sacred, unblemished and transcendent language of music, he deals with the supernatural, the eternally true being.

There is an important section in Natyashastra which deals with the *ouchitya* or the correct proportion of implementing the technique embellishments or any other thing in art and aesthetics. We do not intend to go into the details of this aspect of Indian aesthetics. Who-so-ever interested to know more about it may refer to the Natyashastra. But talking about *ouchitya* is completely relevant at a place where we are discussing about Ustad Bismillah Khan's music, since we should always be sure to find *ouchitya* par excellence in his music. He blends everything in the accurate proportions in order to produce a complete balance in his music. Nothing is short in his performance, nor something is lacking. There is no repetition of phrases or flourishes. His music is crisp, thus perfect, precise and complete.

If you are going to Ustad Bismillah Khan's concert for a single-line-melody meditation, you are mistaken. No, it is not easy to close your eyes and meditate while Ustad Bismillah Khan is performing. He does not give any chance to a *yogi* to muse, nor supports a delirious dreamer. He demands your full attention.

He is a yogi himself, who is creating the vibrations of a grand *sadhana*. You have to be completely awake while listening to him. You have to be mentally prepared to take such an enormous experience. A half-hearted listener or a casual goer to a concert hall might fail to know him, truly. Actually, it is not the instrument-*shehnai*, it is Ustad Bismillah Khan, who reverberates in a concert hall. No wonder that *shehnai* as an individual musical instrument was never played in a classical music conference of India till Bismillah Khan appeared in the scene, and it may not be played anymore as he would be gone. It is a different thing that *shehnai* would be played as usual at the auspicious occasions, but will there be anyone after Ustad Bismillah Khan who will be able to open a music concert with his overpowering music of the *shehnai*? Will there be anybody to bear the flag of the Wizard of *shehnai*, Ustad Bismillah Khan?

2

Benaras

To speak about Bismillah Khan, one must know about Benaras, the ancient city of India which has gifted the world with such a grand musician; the *guru-shishya parampara* or tradition of learning in this country which demands rigorous practice, and flawless devotion towards the teacher and the lessons. One has to understand the inflexible rules and rituals of this tradition, have the knowledge of the ambience in which such traditions raise the favoured sons of *Saraswati*, the Muse, like Khan Sahib Bismillah Khan, the wizard of *shehnai*. One has to know about *shehnai*, which has developed from the insignificant '*pungi*' or '*simha*' of the yesteryears into a dignified musical instrument to whom Khan Sahib has brought world-wide fame. Any description of Bismillah Khan sans accounts of the meandering lanes of Benaras, the stringent codes of a strange teacher-student relationship would be, like playing the *shehnai* without a *sur* and all its other attending instruments.

Benaras or Varanasi, is one of the oldest cities in the world. Benaras the city of light, fervant life and divine bliss; Benaras, the seat of learning, philosophy, religion and performing art, Benaras, a centre for trade and commerce and a paradise of the bullies and thugs has been attracting people from all over the world towards it since times unknown. It is an important and holy town of Hindu pilgrimage. People come here to learn, to think, to meditate and to die, as Benaras is supposed to be the gate-way of heaven.

As the Aryans came to get settled at the northern edge of Benaras, the Rajghat Plateau which overlooks the Ganges, slowly the area became a centre for Vedic learning. The Aryans were called the *Kashis*, and so the name Kashi became popular for the northern part of Benaras. Kashi was known as the city of light, the luminous. The name Benaras which means the Forest of Bliss has its root in the dense and peaceful forests that grew on these glades. Even today patches of green could be spotted all over this old and congested city. Havell in his book 'Benaras, the sacred city' writes describing the picturesque planning of the city with the weaving verdant spots - "If it were not for the temples and the people, it would be easy to imagine oneself to be wandering in an old town of Spain or Southern Italy." The old name Varanasi of the city of Benaras has come out of the union of the two rivers Varuna and Asi (the dry river) that flow here.

The first time I went to Benaras, I was a baby. The only memory I have is that my uncle bought me some toys of wood, and each one of them had a musical instrument in its hands. A set of toys that I happily use as a *barat* procession (people moving in sequence ostentatiously after the bride-groom) during the occasions of my doll's marriage. Thus unconsciously right in my babyhood, I got associated with Kashi and its music world.

We find the name of Kashi in the epics *Mahabharata* and *Ramayana*. Upanishada also talks about Kashi. According to history Benaras was founded sometime in between 1600 B.C. and 800 B.C. This implies that Kashi has been here since the time when the skill of writing human history was not born. But the old city of Kashi was completely destroyed by the Muslim invasions. Especially after the invasion of Qutab-ud-din Aibak, almost all the important temples were destroyed. After the plunder in 1194 the city shifted southwards. Now most of the northern parts of the city are inhabited by the Muslims. The names of the localities are also given after the names of the old Muslim Governors.

Kashi, the Luminous is situated over three hillocks, one of which now contains only the ruins of the old city. It is divided into seven sections with a natural rivulet running towards the Ganges. Previously Kashi was planned in the shape of a chariot but now it looks like a conch. Both these shapes especially the conch is sacred according to Hindu religion. A conch is the oldest *Sushir Vadya* that is used on all occasions of religious ceremonies and worship. Interestingly, *shehnai* also comes from the same category of instruments, Kashi is said to be situated on Shiva's trident. Thus perchance are there the three hillocks, signifying the three prongs of the trident. The holy city is guarded by Lord Shiva and people believe that whoever chooses to die in Kashi gets *Moksha* or Salvation. People from assorted clans and groups all over India and abroad keep thronging this holy place in the hope of getting inner peace and light.

My second visit to Benaras was an excursion, as a member of a Vishwabharati team. If the first visit made me accustomed to the various musical instruments although in toy forms, when I was just a baby, it was during my second visit to Benaras that I had my first grand experience of music when I became actually seriously interested in getting myself trained a dancer.

I distinctly remember, we were taken to hear the Dagar brothers (the elder pair). The *alaap* in *Gaur Sarang* in a strong and majestic pace, in the deep sonorous voice still haunts my memory. Till this date it is my most cherished recollection of listening to *dhrupad*. We went to see the temples and *ghats* of Benaras as a part of sight-seeing. We crossed the Vishwanath *gali* (lane). Little shops and kiosks were packed with teeny-tiny sundries such as *bindis*, colour powder in small brass containers, and small copper utensils used in Hindu ritualistic worship. For a long time I used one such utensil as an ash-tray. Later on I learned that the twin vessels in fish-shape were known as *kosha-kushi.* As a child, born in a freedom-fighter's family with a highly intellectual pedigree, I don't remember having seen my mother ever performing any puja. There was not a single idol in our home. Thus, I was least familiar with these small images and utensils with which any Indian girl would be acquainted. I picked up a little crawling baby made up of *panchadhatu* or five metals, from the Vishwanath *gali.* It was an idol of baby Krishna. I still have it with me. I put it at the place where I keep my teachers' photographs.

An incident which happened after we proceeded towards the temple jaunting and window-shopping, I can not forget till today. I was wearing a white *shalwar-kamiz* with a red *dupatta* (scarf) over it. The atmosphere was of confusion and clamour. I heard people screaming, trying to tell me something. Totally unaware of what I was going to face I tried to understand as to why people were screaming at me. Right then, a tall and hefty man jumped over me, and pushed me back saying - *'mar Jayegi, mar jayegi' i.e.,* she will die, she will die. I saw a black bull - which crossed my body as I fell, down, snatching away my red *dupatta,* it ran away at a furious speed. I was saved but for a bad gash on my cheek. A shop-keeper gave me the first-aid, and said that *Baba* Vishwanath had saved me otherwise I would have been dead. I was upset with my bleeding cheek, and took a detour without a *darshan* of Lord Vishwanath towards the *ghat.* As I climbed up I heard one of the most beautiful voices singing *Puria Dhaneshri.* He was an old man who sat with his eyes closed, and tears trickling down his cheeks, entirely engrossed in his music. I don't know how long I sat there. Later on I was told that he was the legendary singer Bade Ramdasji. I remember the composition I heard till today-

"Langar todi bat nahi jani"

O my beloved I am unaware of thy roads.

I also learnt that directly or indirectly, the entire clan of the *shehnai* players learned from Bade Ramdasji and his disciple Mahadev Mishra in the city of Benaras.

Ever since the Aryan times great and wise souls have been rising from the soil of Kashi. Kashi was called *Brahma Vardhana* or the philosophical lighthead in the ancient past when its philosopher king Ajatshatru brought glory to the city with the glow of his knowledge. There is a kind of enchantment in the air of Benaras that attracts the great scholars, artists, sages and old and ailing people from all strata of the society, like bees swarming round the hive. Some come looking for enlightenment, some in search of the unknown, to wander about here, whereas the old and ailing wait for their mortal ends which they believe would be serene and blessed.

There are twelve *Jyotirlingams* throughout India including Nepal. Each *Jyotirlingam* symbolizes different aspects of the living being. In Benaras where there is one such *Lingam*, Shiva manifests himself in his most affectionate, loving and giving form, consequently the name *Vishwanath* - the Protector of the world is given to him at Kashi. Lord Shiva guards this holy city mounting Kashi on his favourite *trishul*. The *trishul* or the trident is the most significant and ancient concept of asymmetry which is responsible for shaping the Indian philosophy and performing arts. This gives a sprinkling of the secret thoughts of Jo-ha-q of Zen philosophy. It also explains the trinity of all creations that a third power rises from the powers of the union of the two polarities. This is the power which is all powerful. The *tehai* or *tirmaram* in Indian performing art has come into being with its notes in this philosophy.

The exquisite *tehai* with which Bismillah Khan ends his performance gives us the feel of these eternal musical truths, and take the audience to the realms of the divine Spirit. Sadly enough, Aurangzeb destroyed the great Vishwanath temple of Kashi again in 1669. The *Lingam* was hidden in a secret place by a priest who later made a small structure where he kept the *Lingam* and worshipped. The present Vishwanath temple was built by Ahalya Bai in 1777, at the site of the original temple. The largest Muslim population lives close to the temple area today. A fresh crop of settlers who gave birth to the Arabic centres of learning here. It is this deity in the Vishwanath temple that wakes up every morning with the tunes of *shehnai*. Now-a-days only recorded *shehnai* music is played in the temple, as it has become very expensive to maintain a *shehnai*-player. Thanks to Bismillah Khan, it is not only Lord Vishwanath, the whole world today is the listener of *shehnai*. Today, if one wants to hear music of ritualistic back-ground, one has to be at the temple at 11.30 A.M. when the *nadswaram* players of the South bring in procession the holy Ganges water, and raw milk to bathe the deity on behalf of the Rajah of Mysore.

Today with its morning and evening bells tinkling, the incenses burning, *divas* glowing in the temples and at other places; with its arts and artistry; with the incantations and music wafting through the living ether; with the buzz and jostle in the market places and sages and hooligans, Benaras creates a strange atmosphere which is profane and pious, cruel and benign at the same time. This is perhaps how Benaras blends the two polarities to bring out a third and all-powerful power. This is the charm and magic of Benaras that attracts every soul.

Although the bliss of Benaras and the light of Kashi make hearts throb and long for its sight, yet the people here have a curious mentality of spurning the outsiders. In 6th century

B.C. Buddha walked two hundred kms. to reach Kashi after he got his enlightenment in Bodhgaya. He came in search of the five Brahmins who became his first disciples. The contempt of the citizens of Kashi fell on him, and he was forbidden to enter the sacred city. Later Buddha was to reconcile with a settlement in a place called Sarnath which is 4kms. from Kashi, although within the perimeter of Benaras. The arrogance of the *Shaibait* puritanism in this city went to the extent of inventing a new Hindi word-*buddhu* - which means, an ignorant person. The word *buddhu* was formed to mock at Lord Buddha's name. Unfortunately, till today there is no place for Buddhism in Kashi, though Islam has flourished confidently, and most of Kashi is now inhabited by the Muslims.

Almost after ten years after my first two visits, I went to Benaras again with my Guru Siddheswari Devi. It is one of the most cherished memory of my life. It was the first time, I took *"Chillah"*. *Chillah* is a non-stop practice of music of the same pattern for eleven, fifteen or twenty-one days. During the *Chillah,* except for the instances of nature's call, the student singer is required to practice continuously, even while eating. My teacher would constantly feed me with nutritious foods lest I should lose my health. A glass full of milk, filled with pure *ghee,* early in the morning was followed by a glass of juice; afterwards *halwa* cooked in pure *ghee* would be given with a bowl of milk and *jalebi*. The *jalebi* was to be eaten after getting it soaked in the bowl of milk. I used to call my teaher *Ma,* that is mother, and she was an epitome of extraordinary motherly affection to me. As it was difficult for me to consume so much of sweets being unaccustomed to eating so much of them, my teacher would reluctantly make a *parantha,* soaked in *ghee* again. She was an excellent cook. She would bring her little clay oven in our practice room, and cook while supervising my *riaz*. Her most favourite dish was lightly seasoned peas. Her food would exude the warmth of the same love that was woven in her affectionate nature.

My teacher, Siddeshwari Devi was very happy when I successfully finished my *Chillah* on the twenty-first day. She threw a party to all the eminent musicians living in the neighbouring area of Kabir Chauraha. Each house in the locality was sent five *laddoos*. A ruthless and hard task-master, my teacher would take my head fondly in her bosom, weeping ceaselessly, as she would go on saying "You are my true child. So what if you were not born from my womb; *Vishwanath* has given me a strong girl with a firm determination to go through a *Chillah*. You know my girl, till very recently no student would ever get tied a *ganda* by a woman musician and when you tied against all odds I took a vow that I will not deceive you. Whatever I know, I will teach you. I will send you to other masters to learn what is beyond my capability."

It was time for merriment now after the perfect accomplishment of the *Chillah*. I was to go through the normal schedules of practice under the guidance of my exacting teacher from then onwards. I started learning small compositions now. My teacher, overjoyed with my accomplishment took me to the market-place for shopping. She bought me some exquisite, small vessels made of brass for cooking; a set of twenty four bangles on each hand packed with two attractive, matching *kadas* of *lac*; a Banarsi silk *sari* with a suitable blouse, a pair of shoes, and an agreeable tassel to tie in my long braid. She admired my hair and washed them with her own hands in luke warm water.

My guru, was so delighted at my attaining the goal of completing the *Chillah* that her affection knew no bounds. Fondly, she asked me, "What is it that you want as a reward? Moon or star? Say whatever you would like to have?" Her tender eyes bright with radiant smile probed into my secret desires.

"Yes, come out, say." She kept on insisting. "I promise", her voice was dripping with emotion as she continued, "I will give you whatever you wish to have. Is it the *jhumka* of Lalita Bai (Lalita Bai was a singer who lived in a part of Siddheswari Devi's apartment as a tenant) that you were praising?" I was overwhelmed by the assurance and security bestowed by my benevolent teacher. I had never received such kindness before, not even from my own mother. Perhaps this relationship between the teacher and the student is so strong and wonderful that it crossed all the barriers of the worldly bounds. A kinship, a strange union that is more than and above even the blood-relationships. "No, let me not tell you." I replied with a quivery accent, "I know, you won't like it, and I don't wish to lose you as a teacher, *Ma*," adding anxiously. But my teacher knew how to wheedle the truth out of me. At last I gave away the truth whispering in her ears "I wish to see a *"mujra."* Born in Lucknow I had remained always curious about *mujra* as a child. The word was popular there, since Lucknow was the seat of all kinds of professional singing women. The word would intrigue me, but as a young girl, I was forbidden even to utter it. Now as a grown up in my late teens, I thought my self to be quite eligible to witness one. Hence my strange desire, as Benaras was famous for the art of *mujra*.

It was stupid of me to ask my guru for such a thing. I was not even aware at that time of her back-ground. She belonged to the family of professional-singing women. I now understand how much pain I had caused her by disclosing my secret desire. She looked sad, and her face darkened a while. But the arrow had already been shot, and she rose to her feet. She took me to Chowk from Kabir Chauraha in a rickshaw. We climbed the narrow staircase of a house there, and reluctantly got into a rather large showroom of Banarsi *saris*. An elderly gentleman ran towards *Amma*, my teacher, the master of the art of *Thumri* singing. He welcomed her congratulating for her recent President's award, the Padmashri. We were offered cold drinks, and *paan* - a typical custom of Benaras. Afterwards holding the gentleman's right hand my teacher implored, "You will have to save my honour. I have come to beg you for something." The gentleman was overwhelmed. He answered, "But surely, I know, it will be my honour to serve you. We are all very proud of you, and your achievements. Please tell me what's it that you want from me?" Looking at me fondly, and patting on my head she replied, "I want my room just for a day." She introduced me and told the gentleman. *"Ye bade baap ki beti hai. Galti se vada kar baithe, aab dharmsankat ki baat hai."* (She hails from a well-known family. Unknowingly, I have made the mistake of making a promise to her, and now my honour is at stake.) She repeated her request, and the man happily agreed.

The next day was a Saturday. The gentleman of the showroom packed his bundles of *saris,* removed the sitting arrangements, closed the almirahs which had mirrors on the other side, and kept his promise. He also assured my teacher that there would be no other *mujrah* in Benaras that evening, as all famous singers and dancers would willingly come to pay salutation to Siddheshwari Devi who had brought great glory to the city.

A peculiar trait of the Indian society is that it never gives any respect to great people as long as they are available easily, in the neighbourhood. Local artists, even if they are world-known are neglected, even slighted and mocked at, but soon as they leave their native place, the people at home start regarding them great. My teacher had to suffer endless humiliations as long as she lived in Benaras, but now that she lived there no more, the people were anxious to exalt her. They were ready to recognize her as their own. Khansahib Bismillah Khan also has to bear the same fate. While the whole world drank the nectar of the tuneful music of his *shehnai*, and honoured him, the local people of Benaras barely noticed the beatitude of the maestro's presence there. He roams through the contracted lanes of Kashi, blowing on his *shehnai* weaving magical melodies, while the bustle of Kashi goes on unmindful of him, and his divine music.

The atmosphere of *mujrah* was articulately and adroitly recreated as the mirrors blazed in the light and the sound of music echoed in the ether. It was a *mujrah* organized by my teacher exclusively for me. The chandeliers hanged from the ceiling pouring out flickering specks of sparkles, the *gajra* man with his flowers at his place, the *paan-wala* with the bunches of the famous betel leaves - preparing the fragrant Banarsi paan, with *kattha,* lime and all other spices and the *sarangi* with its whinning notes spinning through the dreamy evening all created the euphonious ambience of *mujrah* of thirty years back. Such an atmosphere of mellifluous music is no more where the dancer yields to the unblemished rhythm of the *tabla* improvising intricate gestures. It truly was the atmosphere in which the *shehnai*-wizzard Bismillah Khan grew up, learning cadence and cadenza, soprano and bass, all nuances of vocal music from the professional signing women. The intricacies of tones that later produced from his *shehnai*.

The evening stretched from 8 P.M. to 4.30 A.M. My teacher with her admirable wit found a way of presenting me to the performing artists. She tied a turban round my head, and announced to the participants, "A *Seth* (a wealthy man) from Delhi. You have to perform for him." It was a memorable evening. Every body enjoyed as though participating in a drama. There were six outstanding performers in the show. Each contributed with admirable skill and talent to add to the splendour of the show. The *bhav* of Alaknanda, the elder sister of Sitara Devi was brilliant. I have not seen such acumen of *'bhav'* in any other dancer till date. It was as though I was looking back in time, retracing the dreams of the past, riding on the magical tunes and rhythm. I understood how rich were our traditions, and then why should they be lost?

Now it was time to leave Benaras. My teacher Siddheshwari Devi was the most sought after singer of the country in those years and she had series of concerts to attend. I was to accompany her. This was a rare privilege bestowed on me. Normally, only the children or close relations of the great masters would accompany them; but the magic of the *guru-shishya parampara* can break the shackles of all existing customs. It is an arcane relationship which ties the teacher and the student with unknown cords or perhaps with sweet and unforgettable chords of music. It is this *guru-shishya Parampara* which nurtured and nourished Bismillah Khan as he grew up to be the celebrated master of music under the guidance of his noble *Ustad* Ali Bux, whom he still talks about with tears in his eyes.

I carefully planned the reservation schedule of my teacher's concert tour. She was very unwilling to let me go to the railway station for the reservation when I insisted upon going alone. Benaras being a crowded commercial city and a holy place also where *goondaism*, kidnapping and flesh-trading flourished in full swing, it is not a safe place for a solitary girl, and so she was worried. She gave her consent finally, when I constantly urged being confident as an educated person. I hailed a rickshaw, and went to the railway station. It took me two hours to get the reservations done. I found my teacher waiting for me at the same place near the door where I left her when I came back. Such was the concern of my teacher, my *Ma*, for me. Khan Sahib had expressed about same kind of concern of his *Ustad* while talking about Ali Bux.

Sadly enough, till today this *goondaism*, cheating and even murders thrive in the sacred city of Benaras without any scruples. The confusions and commotions created by the local hooligans here could go to such an extent that a new comer in the city could be puzzled and afraid. Benaras is a city of the labyrinths of narrow and crooked lanes and alleys. One can not guess what exists inside these lanes viewing them from the periphery. Such planning was designed in order to save the area from intrusions and invasions. In the olden days the local *goondas* and *dadas* used to guard the lanes, and each lane used to have a gate at its entrance. The local hooligans of Benaras are famed for their mischief as well as vindication and power. During the British Raj the Maharaja of Benaras Chet Singh was house-arrested by Warren Hastings when he refused to pay taxes; but the Rajah escaped (1781) making a ladder of his turban from the window of his palace. Later he was helped by the local rowdies and the British had to face a strong opposition. It is the *kund* of Chet singh that was later on declared as Victoria Park. A statue of Queen Victoria that was erected here is now being kept in the National Museum, Delhi. On one side of this park, now live the Muslim citizens of Benaras. It is called Benia Bagh. Sarai harrna, a place in Benia Bagh is the locality where Bismillah Khan, the *shehnai* maestro has spent 80 years of his life in the house of his maternal ancestors. Unlike other glamorous singers and musicians who have left their ancestral homes to settle down in the luxurious bunglows of the metropolitan cities of India, Khan Sahib has preferred to live in Kashi where the Ganges flows singing serene melodies to his yearning heart which is forever thirsty for this peaceful and miraculous music.

It is said that the world renowned film director Satyajit Ray became puzzled by the behaviour of the over-zealous crowd in Benaras, while shooting for his film, 'Jai Baba Bholanath'. The police failed to control the unruly mass, and the great director thought of changing the location.

The local rowdies came to his rescue. The next day they kept the roads all clear of various traffics as well as crowds. Thus, the world famous director could shoot for his film without changing the location. Such is the graciousness of the *goondas* of Benaras. Still it is true that the travellers suffer in the hands of the *goondas* and thugs in this city. The law and order in this place also get disturbed being at the mercy of these outlaws.

Thus, although after the independence, all other grand arts and artistry died away, the one art-form which still flourishes ardently in Benaras, is this *goondaism*. Thanks to the modern era politicians, aristocracy, and anti-social activists who are the patrons of this art, and who zealously guard the thugs and bullies of Benaras whose fame is no less than the fame of Lord *Vishwanath* in Kashi. "Have you ever heard that a musician has killed some one ... or two musicians fighting a duel in other form than with their music?" We don't need *dadas*, we need *riaz*, the master Bismillah Khan of Benaras of wise and great souls Kashi never had any dearth. Many were born in the city where as others came guided by the luminosity of the city. Of all the eminent *gharanas* of Indian classical music the Benaras *gharana* today is the foremost, especially the *thumri* and Benaras *baj tabla*. The city is the seat of the grand *tabla* players of the Sahai family who are the pioneers of the Benaras *baj style*. Sharda Sahai is the torch-bearer of this style today. He is settled in England now. The great Kanthe Maharaj's legendary son Kishan Maharaj still lives in the Kabir Chauraha of Benaras. His disciples all over the world are playing brilliant *tabla* music. The great Shanta Prasad, an out-standing tabla player, still lives in Benaras. His son Kumar is now associated with the A.I.R. Varanasi. The grand-master of *tabla*, Anokhe Lal, who is remembered for his exquisite thrumming and thumps of music also hails from the Banaras *gharana*. The Hindu school of *sarangi* players emerged from this sacred land of music, among whom Shivaji Maharaj and Gopal Mishra stand prominently. Even today Hanuman Mishra teaches innumerable students the Benaras style of singing. His sons Rajan Mishra and Sajan Mishra are well-known for their *khayae gayaki*. The *kathak* school has the doyen of *kathak* Sitara Devi. Sunayana Hazarilal has also earned a special place in the hierarchy of *kathak* dances. But Lord *Vishwanath* waits only for the music of *shehnai* to wake up.

From the Vedic times Benaras is well-known as a centre for learning and education. There used to be continuous exchanges of scholars, philosophers and intellectuals between Benaras and the two great Universities of India of the yesteryears, the Nalanda which was situated in Bihar and Takshila, now in Pakistan. Huen Tsang, the great Buddhist scholar and traveller mentioned Benaras as an eminent centre for learning in his description of India. Today there are 300 various institutions of education and learning in Benaras. There is the centre for Tibetan studies in Sarnath, Jain Vidyalaya, as four stalwarts of Jain religion were born in this religious city before Mahavira. Also there are the centres for Sanskrit learning. Sanskrit *pathshalas* and Vishva Vidyalaya which keep alive the ancient tradition of learning of the Vedic era. The *Shastri* titles are conferred from these institutions of Sanskrit learning. We come to know about the names of Shri M.M. Gangadhar Shastri of Benaras who was called the walking library, and Shri M.M. Bapudeva Shastri, who became the Honorary fellow of the Royal Society. Benaras is also known for Ayurveda. It is said that Dhanvantari, the father of Indian Medicine was born as the king of Kashi. He taught medicine to his disciple Sushruta who discovered plastic surgery. Thus the city has become an important place for Ayurvedic education too. With the arrival of the Muslims, the centres for Arabic, Persian and Islamic studies have also come up to adorn Benaras's world of learning and education. The Kashi Vidyapith was built in order to oppose the British system of education. But above and ahead of all these centres of education the Banaras Hindu University shines like a bright star. It was established by Pandit Madan Mohan Malaviya in 1917. The Banaras Hindu University represents the true picture of the intellectual life of Benaras. An amusing story about Pt. Madan Mohan Malaviya goes like this, he refused to move into Kashi, because he did not want to have liberation, as he would say he had much to do in his next lifetime. Dr. Rai Anand Krishna, the art historian taught in the Banaras Hindu University till he retired. His father alone, gathered the well-known art collections in the Bharat Kala Bhavan.

But then music can not be learned in any institution. You need an honest guru, an *Ustad* who breaths the knowledge in your ears, who opens your inner eyes. Benaras is the hallowed place where the virtuous *guru-shishya parampara* has been blooming from time immemorial. Guru or the teacher is the embodiment of learning imparting knowledge to the *shishya* or disciple. It is a system of learning under which Bismillah Khan was trained by his *Ustad*, Ali Bux.

It is here in Kashi, Patanjal the illustrious grammarian founded his Yoga School of Philosophy, and wrote his great treatise in the 2nd century B.C. The mystic-poet and spiritualist Kabir belonged to Kashi. The hundreds of verses that he wrote here, now reverberate in the air of Kashi as famous *bhakti-sangeets* that are full of metaphysical meanings, adding divine resplendence to the aura of this religious city. Although Kabir worked and preached in Kashi he chose to stop his mortal mission away from Kashi, as he did not want to take any undue favour from God by taking his last breath in the place. He trusted his own divine light and halted his earthly toils in an insignificant village Magahar, where his followers found only a basket of flowers under his blanket, not a dead-body.

Kabir had to suffer immensely in the hands of the citizens of Kashi, and its rulers. The contempt of Kashi revealed itself in a different manner in his case. Buddha was not allowed to enter Kashi; but for Kabir there were insults, beatings and endless cruel tests, mainly because he belonged to the Julaha community, a lower caste in the Hindu society. Tulsidas, the *bhakti*-poet (1543-1623) had also to go through his share of testings, as he wrote his great Ramcharitmanas meditating and contemplating on the banks of the river Ganges. Since Ramayana was an ancient epic written in the scripts of the gods, Sanskrit, no one was permitted to write the Ramayana in Hindi, the language of the common people. The priests in the temple of Kashi kept the Ramcharitmanas of Tulsidas beneath all other Sanskrit texts at night, but by the morning Tulsi's Ramcharitmanas had reached the top of all the books that were above it. Such is the wonder and mystery of Kashi. One has to pass through trials in order to get assimilated in the flow.

Not only as a centre for learning and varied artforms, Benaras has been famous as a nucleus of trade and commerce also since the ancient eras. Banarasi *saris* with their exquisite embroidered patterns are well-known all over the world. Benarsi *paan* (betel) with its unique tastes of spices, brass and brocade items and various handicrafts thrive here with extraordinary fervour. The narrow and winding lanes of Benaras are all crowded with little shops and kiosks where endless assorted items are sold to the eager shoppers and customers day and night.

The elegance of the splendid filigri work of brocade and the relish of the scented juice of *paan* that are famous in Benaras, we get a feel of them in the delicate and fragile rendering of *shehnai* music of Bismillah Khan. His *shehnai* bestows on our souls the immortal nectar of life, and feeds our thirsty hearts with immaculate doses of aesthetic juice which is full of sweet aroma and joy like the subtle betel-nut in the Benarsi *paan*.

The culture of Benaras is of *mauj* and *masti i.e.,* festivities, gaiety and living a full and hearty life of inner calm and bliss, again shows the strange contradictory character of the holy city which makes one wary and impulsive simultaneously. Throughout the year the city throbs with the joyous celebrations of innumerable functions and festivities. Various performing arts of India form a significant part of these festivals from times unknown. Music has been weaving through the aura of Benaras from the time of the *Aryans* when the *mantras* in the forms of musical verses were chanted during *yajnas*. The *khayal* of *Sadrang* and *Adrang*, the Jaunpuri and Hussaini *todi* of the yesteryears still echo in the air here. The Burhwa Mangal and the Gulab Bari festival express the real mood of *mauj* in Benaras which is devoid of all clashes of clans, castes, communities and nationalities. They glow with the light of love and pure brother-hood.

Affluent people like Motichand and Kishore Raman were the wanted guests in the Burhwa festival. Talking about Kishori Raman, Bismillah Khan says that he was a true *raees* (a royal man) with a sprawling house, brocades and silk and all other accessories of aristocracy. A connoisseur of music Kishori Raman died in 1894. Even today Bismillah Khan's son plays *shehnai* in the famous music-room of his house. Once upon a time in the lost past all great musicians of India played in the music-room of Kishori Raman. Pandit Ravi Shankar flew specially to play during the occasion when Kishori Raman passed away.

Khan Sahib Bismillah Khan describes the Burhwa Mangal festival as the *kajri* festival. It used to take place during the rainy season when the women swing on the swings. The rich and wealthy people would organize the function. All kinds of delicacies of gourmet refinement would be cooked for the guests and the participants in the festival. Mangoes of delectable tastes also would be served. The well-known women performing artists of the yester years sang in the festival. Khan Sahib relates that as it would begin to rain lightly over the festival arena the famous singers like Rasoolan Bai, Batoolan Bai and others would start singing their peculiar chorus, slowly swaying on the swings. This singing on the swings was the characteristic feature of the *kajri* festival. The master of Bismillah Khan, *Ustad* Ali Bux used to play his unique *shehnai* in this festival. He would produce one line of a lyrical composition announcing the beginning of the function, and the famed singers would follow him one after another singing in sequence as the melody would again come back to Ali Bux to be played. Starting from morning the festivities would go on till about 1.30 A.M. Afterwards people used to eat and drink *Thandai*, the famous intoxicating drink of Benaras, and make merry as they would return bathed and washed. It was customary to give all the money collected during these festivals to Ali Bux, the *Ustad* of Khan Sahib. Thus, the nature of *mauj* in the culture of Benaras explains the cause of *masti* in life here. It is from such happy and selfless human union the inner bliss and tranquility are born.

Listening to Bismillah Khan gives a distinctive feeling of bliss. It is a strange elation, and one fails to understand if it is bliss or gaiety. We travel with the music of the maestro to the same realms where he reached during the early years of his training period, when the Sadhu, the Adepti appeared to bless him, and said, "*Mazaa karega, mazaa karega.*" *i.e.*, you will enjoy bliss. It is the gift of that supernatural bliss which Bismillah Khan is dispensing to our clamorous world till today.

The era of contemporary perception started in Benaras with the birth of Bharatendu Harishchandra (1850) - Father of contemporary literature and well-known playwright, Bharatendu Harishchandra used to trade in snuff and tobacco. Though he came from a business family, yet his house is still an eminent landmark of literature in the city of Benaras. His association with the professional singing women made him infamous during his lifetime; but it is from these associations he gained his insight of human tragedy, love and ecstasy. A valuable perception which his literature never ceases to reflect.

During the last part of the 19th century a flock of great souls descended in Benaras to bring light to the world with their diverse thinking, skill and wisdom. Jai Shankar Prasad - Father of *Chhayavadi* poetry, Hazariprasad Dwivedi (1907), the literary giant and professor of Benaras Hindu University emerged in Benaras to adorn its rich and splendid cultural atmosphere. Also, the new stars rose in the sky of music—Ravi Shankar, the great *sitar* maestro whose illustrious brother Udai Shankar made Indian classical dance well-known in the world, and the wizard of *shehnai* Bismillah Khan arrived in Benaras to open new vistas for Indian music. The time was ripe now for Benaras, the city of piety and notoriety, where harmony hides beneath chaos to gain not national, but international fame.

3

Sushir Vadya

One of the oldest treatise on the performing arts of India—Natya Shastra (2C.B.C.) identifies, and clarifies the various musical instruments into four categories, (1) *Ghana Vadya* (Ideophonic instruments), (2) *Avanddha Vadya* (Memobrophonic instruments) (3) *Sushir Vadya* (Aerophonic instruments or aerophones), and (4) *Tat Vadya* (String instruments). Interestingly enough, eminent musicologists, and ethno-musicologists from all over the world have not been able to identify a fifth category. *shehnai* comes under the third category of *Sushir Vadya*. The *Sushir Vadya* variety of musical instruments are played through lips with various blowing techniques.

The lip-voiced instruments in India remained unimportant for a long time. Most of these instruments emerged as folk instruments, and they have assorted classes and kinds. The use of these instruments was mainly confined to the temples, family worships, religious ceremonies, processions and pageantries. The tonal quality of these instruments is variable, depending on the size and shape of the pipe used. Most of these instruments are capable of producing voluminous sounds - from deep bass to piercing, shrill notes. The tonal dynamics and pitch of the instruments are controlled by the movements of the lips and by the pressure used in blowing. The increase in the size will make the tonal quality deeper and with the decrease in the size, the tonal quality will change with the heightening of the pitch.

The most popular *Sushir Vadya* as the earliest natural instrument, must have been the "conch", which was, and still is associated through out the country with the temples, worship-rituals as well as with all the social ceremonies like engagements, marriages, the ceremonial entry of the bride into the groom's house, before the wedding-night, at the time of child-birth, first rice-eating ritual of a child, the sacred thread ceremony etc. The *shehani* from the beginning too has remained associated with all these auspicious occasions. Ironically, while the Brahmin blew on the conch during the sacred ceremonies and rituals, the people, who belonged to the lower caste, and were not allowed to enter the house, would play *shehnai* from outside the courtyard. Although the music of the *shehani* was necessary during the ceremonies and the rituals, the people who played them were debarred.

The folk variety of *shehnai* is found throughout the hill region as *pungi*. Its counterpart is called *simha* or *singha*. The posection of the society using these instruments essentially dealt with snakes, and they were snake-worshippers. The *pungi*, originally was of only 8 inches in size. Slowly the seven holes were introduced to manipulate the melodic expression. Over the centuries it emerged as an important temple instrument. By now, the size of the pipe has increased upto 13"-16".

Shehnai has grown from the simple "*singha*" or "*pungi*" to the "*narsimha*" or "*narsingha*" with the introduction of a fret. Finally, with the addition of a complicated use of frets and complex playing technique through the development of fingering and lip placements, it became the "*shenai*", as we know it today. When a fret called dong which grows among the weeds called `*narkat*' was added to the pipe, it came to be known as *Narsimha*. *Narsimha* players were employed to play this instrument as a daily ritual of temple activity.

Thus it acquired a place in the temple. And because of its association with the temple, the *shehnai* acquired an auspicious status.

Recent portrait of Khan Saheb before leaving for his Iran tour

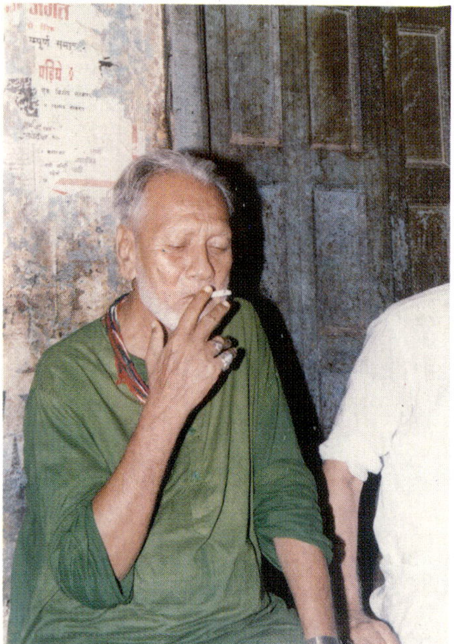

The moods...

Bismillah Khan singing in front of Karbala

Elder brother, a guiding spirit and childhood partner, Shamsuddin; whose death left Khan Saheb a lonely person

Balaji's Mandir the sideroom of the Balaji temple
Inset: Jadau Mandir of Benaras where Bismillah practised as a child and had darshan of Balaji

Bismillah Khan playing at a concert

Playing at a marriage, Brother Shamsuddin and Kamruddin (Bismillah Khan)

An Archival Photograph with the galaxy of superstars of 50's, with India's first President, Dr. Rajendra Prasad. Second from the left Bismillah Khan, Kishan Maharaj, Krishna Rao, Shankar Pandit, Pt. Ravi Shankar, Ali Akbar Khan, Ustad Hafiz Ali Khan, Pandit Omkar Nath Thakur, Kesarbai Kelkar, Ustad Alaudin Khan, and Sumitra Charatram.
(Photograph Courtesy: Ustad Amjad Ali Khan)

Young Bismillah receiving Padma Bhushan from President Zakir Hussain

Khan Saheb playing at a concert

Nand Lalji, one of the outstanding Shehnai players during the days of Ustad Ali Bux

Ustad Ali Bux, Bismillah's teacher

Deshikottam (D.Litt.) Vishwa Bharati University

Highest honour for an artist: Bismillah's Padma Vibhushan

Khan Saheb playing with a silver shehnai specially made, during Moharram

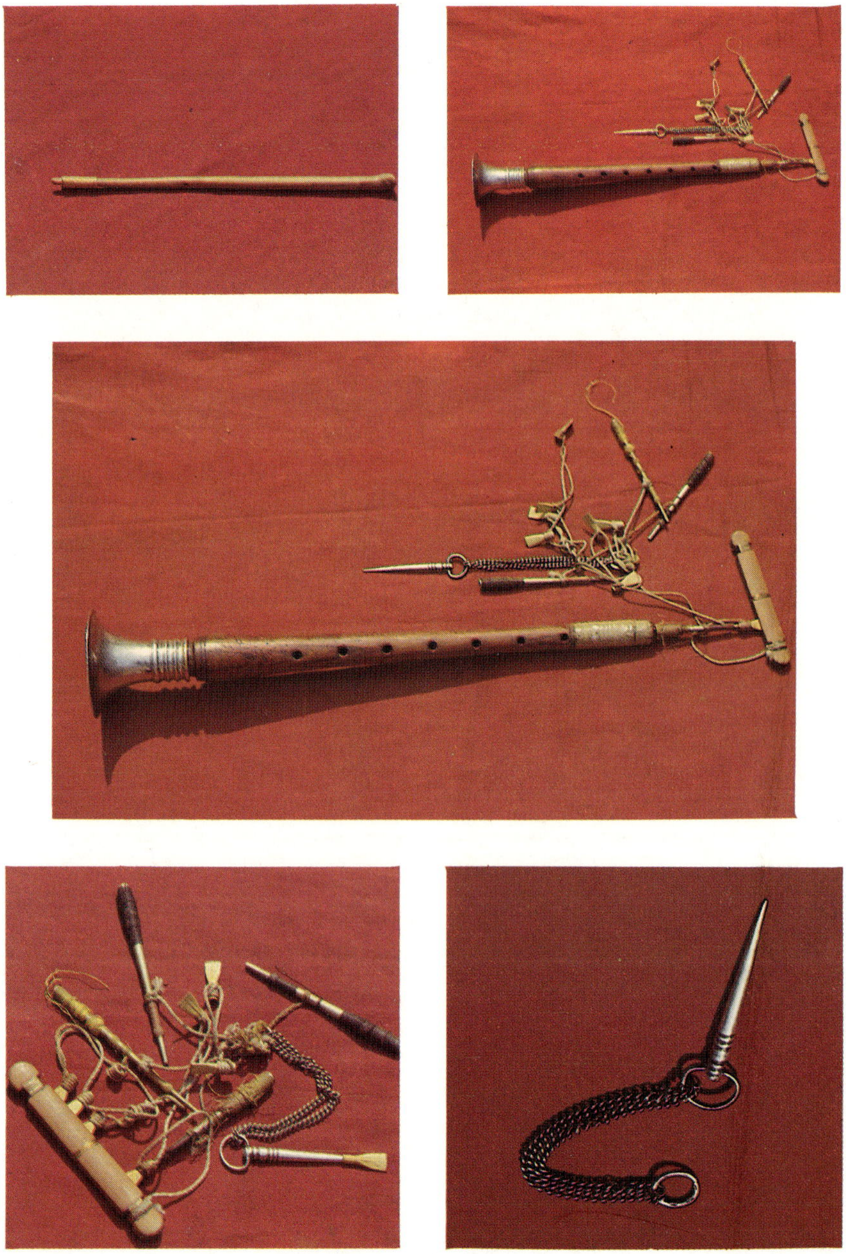

Shehnai, *Pyala, Khazana, Nali*

4

Shehnai

HISTORY

The popular story about the origin of the *shehnai* is told by the eminent Hindu players of the professional *shehnai* player families. The amusing anecdote goes like this: Though the *shehnai* or *'narsimha'* was played in various temples, and was supported by the princely estates, yet in Delhi people played the high-pitched *'pungi'*. The *'pungi'* was the earlier, crude form of the *shehnai*. This instrument, because of its shrill sound quality, was banned by Aurangzeb and came to be known as *'napili'*, a distortion of the original word *'napaak'* (inauspicious). Even today a section of people in the society call the *shehnai* *'nafiri'*.

Afterwards, a barber of the professional musicians family, who had access to the royal residence, worked hard to improve the tonal quality of the instrument. He selected a wood which had a natural hollow stem and used it as the pipe of the *'pungi'*. The size of the instrument now became longer and broader than before. As he carved out seven holes on the body of the instrument, an impressive, sonorous tonal quality was obtained which was far better than the shrill and piercing notes of the *'pungi'*. He carried the new instrument to the emperor's palace and played before the royalty. Immensely pleased about the fresh tonal quality, the Shah enquired about its name. The barber, who in Indian language is called the *'nai'*, quickly took the Benaras version of the name of the instrument-*senai*. But the Shah too was no less prompt in correcting the barber, pointing out that the instrument was born in his royal chamber and should be named *'shahnai'*-the emperor and the barber. Thus the instrument acquired a new name-*shahnai* or *shehnai*.

According to Bismillah Khan, the *shehnai* has its roots in Iran or Persia. Haquim Bu Ali Saina of Iran discovered the *shehnai*. A *haquim* is a doctor in Arabic. In old Iran, according to a strange custom a *haquim* had to be a competent singer. To obtain the licence for practice *haquim* would have to sing before the royalty. The licence would be given only to a good singer. Bu Ali had a flat voice, incapable of producing musical notes. He failed to get a licence for years together due to his awkward voice. He was a very good *haquim*, but his voice was the only hurdle. Bu Ali Saina thought of an idea. He took a piece of wood, made a canal through it by drilling, pierced seven holes over it, made reeds, and blowed on it. The instrument produced beautiful musical tones. He practised on the instrument for some time. As the day for obtaining the licence came, he entreated the Shah to allow him to perform from behind a curtain. The Shah gave his permission. Bu Ali played his instrument from behind the curtain. The Shah and the people in the court were astonished to hear the marvelous music of Bu Ali's instrument. He passed his examination and obtained the certificate to practice as a *haquim*. Thereafter, everybody came to know about the instrument that Bu Ali Saina played to get his licence. Many people learned from Bu Ali Saina the skill of playing the instrument. It was named *'sena'* after Haquim Bu Ali Saina's name. Later on, the instrument came to Peshawar with travellers and became *'tota'* (a long pipe). The *tota* travelled to reach Punjab, and then to Delhi. In Delhi it was called the *'nafiri'* or the *'zafila'*. As the instrument reached Benaras, it acquired the name *'shehnai'*.

But the original *shehnai* players in this country were zealously guarded and patronised by the Hindu royalties who employed them invariably in their temples. The *shehnai* players were later exchanged between the royalties. The Shah of Delhi sent his brilliant *shehnai* player Chhote Khan, as a gift to the Nawab of Lucknow. Chhote Khan, who was of Afghan origin, was one of the most outstanding *shehnai*-players. He improved the instrument, and played it with exceptional skill. The Nawab of Lucknow forced a marriage with the sister of the royal family of Benaras. Thus, a large section of Benaras ghat was gifted by the Maharaja of Benaras to the Nawab. The gift stretched from 'Assi *ghat*' to 'Shivalaye *ghat*' which was later on known as Nawabganj. With the Nawabs Chhote Khan also migrated to Benaras.

A popular story goes on like this, Chhote Khan would play his instrument from this side of the river, and the Maharaja would listen to it from Ramnagar, which was on the other side of the river where the king had his royal palace. The Hindu *shehnai* players who through centuries direct descendents of the families learned, taught and spread the art of *shehnai* playing throughout the country, imbibed a great deal of technique from Chhote Khan. The major disciple of Chhote Khan was Tahal Lal. The descendents of this family, the cousins, and grandchildren and great grandchildren got employment all over the country wherever the Hindu Rajahs maintained a temple, for example in Cooch Behar, Darbhanga and Nepal.

The other contemporary stalwart among the professional *shehnai* players was Gauri Shankar, whose children and grand-children till this date either play *shehnai* or are eminent flute players. Nandlal, who was from a Hindu family had a chance to get trained by Chhote Khan. His main teachers of classical vocal music were from the well known Hindu family of musicians of Bade Ramdasji. Shri Nandlal in his own time acquired great fame, but he was totally non-ambitious, and did not like the idea of leaving Benaras. He remained mainly in the domain of U.P.

Nandlal and Gauri Shankar were the contemporaries of the great Muslim *shehnai* players Allan and Vilayatu of Benaras. These two well-known *shehnai* players trained two of their nephews- Shamsuddin and Qamruddin or Bismillah Khan. Both the brothers became great *shehnai* players. Unfortunately, Shamsuddin died an untimely death, which disturbed the group. But the younger brother with his unswerving perseverance and genius conquered the world with the miraculous sound of the music of his *shehnai*. Thus, he turned the fate of this ordinary instrument, so that it has now become one of the most important classical instruments of India.

THE INSTRUMENT

Today *shehnai* is made out of seasoned Burma teak or *Sagwan*, chiselled step by step, till it acquires the desired width of the *shehnai*. Afterwards, it is carefully drilled from the broader side of the *shehnai* to the side from where it is played. The starting point acquires an half-inch spring and the end-point where the fret is inserted of a hollow weed called, *dong*, narrows down to 4 mm. approximately. The broader part—which originally was carved out from wood, and later on was converted into brass, is specially cast for the *shehnai* players by the brass-ware artisans. The whole instrument takes the length of 15 and 1/2". Now, the whole length is divided into three portions. The front portion which is called the '*pyala*' is made of brass, and measures 3-4 *churis* (screws) seven fingers make the middle portion, and five fingers the last fraction. The first fragment is left out, and the last two parts are equally divided by pirecing seven holes in them.

Initially, the instrument would have a bamboo nozzle, but

slowly a brass nozzle measuring 4"-6" has come into being complying with the needs. On top of the nozzle, a weed fret would be fixed, and with the help of the lips and jaws air is blown to produce the required sound. The names of the various parts of the instrument that is used today are as follows:

(a) *Pyala* (the front portion or mouthpiece which measures 3-4 *churis*).

(b) The major trunk of the instrument with the seven holes.

On top is the *'nali'* which is the brass section of 4"-6". The player keeps two *'nalis'* with him, one small and another big. They are used according to the change of pitch. The *'nali'* is called *"dandi"* in Delhi. Above that is the *'patoor'* made out of a wild grass reed which rows over the banks of the river Sone in Bihar. This wild grass weed is called *'dong'*, an abundance of these weeds are found in Dumraon, Bihar, where Bismillah Khan was born. The tender reeds of *'dong'* are found, growing among the hard reeds of a weed called *'narkat'*. This *'patoor'* gets wet and soggy after some time of playing. The player keeps at least two *'patoors'* tied in a string which is again fixed in a bamboo rack called *'chapeel'*. This rack is made of bamboo pieces of two inches in size tied together at two ends, and at the centre and in between area the *'patoors'* are fixed to keep them in shape. The player keeps two *chapeels* with him. Along with the *'patoors'* hangs a silver needle which is used to clear the nozzles of the *'patoors'* time and again. All these small pieces that hang down the *shehnai* of the player are together called *'khazana'*. The whole instrument of the *shehnai* with all its parts is called the *saaz*.

The *'patoor'* is approximately of one inch in length. A thread is tied at the centre of this hollow reed in order to prevent the saliva from trickling inside the main instrument.

THE PLAYING TECHNIQUE

As the player closes all the six holes from one to six, leaving the last, the bottom hole open, it gives the tonic *'sa'*. Just half of the second hole along with the first one is opened to get the *'komal re'*, when the second hole is completely opened, We get *'shuddha re'*.

The third hole is half opened to get the *'komal gandhar'*. The third hole fully opened gives the *'sudha ga'*. Blowing hard through the fourth hole gives the *'madhyam'* and *'teebra madhyam'*. The fifth hole manipulates the *'pancham'*. The sixth hole half opened gives the *'komal dhaivat'*, and fully opened it gives the *'shudha dhaivat'*. The seventh hole half opened creates the *'komal nishad'*, fully opened gives *'shuddha nishad'*. When the player blows hard through all the nozzles - he gets *taar sa*.

The most difficult thing is to bring out the lower octave. By playing the seventh hole closing all the other holes, the player brings out the *'nishad'*, (*ni*) and then with the technique of blowing the *'dhaivat'* and *'pancham'* is created. There are no natural provision within the instrument to go beyond this which is a great limitation. The instrument can not go below this range.

ACCOMPANYING INSTRUMENTS

1. *THE 'SUR' OR 'DAMKASH'*

It is identical as the *shehnai*. Only the seven holes would be blocked with wax. A constant droning tone that accompanies the main player is obtained from the *'sur'*. Keeping the holes in the body of the instrument is important for the *'sur*-player'. The holes on the main trunk help to obtain a better tonal quality.

2. *THE DUGGAD*

The membrophonic instrument played with the *shehnai*, is

called the *duggad*. It is a smaller version of the *'nagada'*. The *shehnai* player would be accompanied by the *nagada* player in the past. Gradually, *nagada* was discarded due to its loud sound, *duggad* is smaller in size and produces lesser sound. Like the *tabla* the *duggad* is a pair of drums, the left hand side drum is called the *'bayan'* and the right hand side drum is called the *'jeel'*.

The drum at the right hand side is a small earthen pot with a stretched membrophone at the top and a thread at the bottom. It has a lead (*syahi*) treatment on the membrophone which resembles the system of the *'tabla'*. This drum is called the *'jeel'*.

The *'bayan'* of the *'duggad'* is a little taller than the other drum, and is also made out of clay. It has the *'syahi'* spread inside the membrophone. The stretched membrophone on the earthen pot is tied with a rope.

The combination of the *'bayan'* and the *'jeel'* was originally called the *'khurdak'*. Later it has come to be known as *'duggad'*. *duggad* makers are of *'mirasi'* community. They live in Delhi, Amroha and Aligarh. A major section of the makers of such membrophonic instruments are from *'gauraiya'* community.

Many *shehnai* players have begun to use *tabla* instead of the *'duggad'* with them now-a-days. The membrophonic instruments played with the *shehnai* are peculiar in themselves. Their percussion impacts give the same raw and musty feels of the rain drenched earth, forests, flowing streams and undulating waves in the ocean which the music of the *shehnai* itself gives.

3. *MANJIRA*

Originally, the *shehnai* player was accompanied by a *'manjira'* player also. *Manjiras* are two brass plates made out of bell metals. A clanging sound is procured by striking the plates with each other. The *manjira* player too would sit at the right hand side of the main performer, but now-a-days an electronic device called *'surpeti'* is used instead of *'manjiras'*. Today many *shehnai* players even take a *'swara mandal'*, a kind of harp-like cardeophonic instrument.

4. The main *shehnai* player is accompanied by two more *shehnai* players, who are called the *'jodaits'* or *'joridars'*. They sit on both the sides of the main performer.

THE CONCERT SITTING POSITIONS

From the day when the *shehnai* was played in the *'nahabat khana'*, till today the sitting positions of the performers are as follows:

From left to right-the *manjira* player or the *'sur-peti'*, *joridar*, main performer, behind the main performer the *'sur'* player, *joridar* in the same row as the main performer and finally the *'duggad'* player.

VENUE OR THE STAGE

In India, the architecture of royal palaces have been influenced by the compulsion of erecting a *'nahabat khana'* above the entrance to the court-yard. A stair-case, specially erected to reach the platform above the entrance would be placed in between the outer and inner gate of the main entrance. This platform above the gate has various names, such as *baradari*, *nahabat khana* and *roshan chowki*. The platform is again covered by the canopy like arches. As the sun rises, the *shehnai* players, waking up the Gods are seen in a silhouette at the eastern corner, facing the Gods to the western side. This is the arrangement, be it in the courtyard or in a temple. Today, whether in an auditorium or in a raised stage the sitting position of the orchestra remains the same.

DRESS

A *shehnai* player and his team, since it is customary, whether they are playing for Gods or royalty, invariably wear a handgear, an ordinary cap or *topi*. In summer a cotton *topi* and a woolen *topi* in winter, as they always perform in the open air. They wear *'achkans'*- long black coats which go with tight or loose *pyjamas*. On very special occasions, according to the custom of the region the *shehnai* player wears a turban. When a *shehnai* team is performing for a wedding ceremony, every member of the team wears brocade coats (*achkan*), above cotton *pyjamas* of the same colour. The cap that goes with such grand dresses is also made of the same material.

THE INSTRUMENT MAKERS

Unlike other classical instruments, there are no communities as such which make the instrument of *shehnai*. Generally, the carpenters who are specialised in preparing the pipe of the *'hookah'* are the instrument makers for the *'shehnai'* players, the reason being they are well conversant and have the necessary tools and knowhow to carve out a nozzle in a seasoned wood. Once the wood, generally Burma teak, or *Shesham* that are used for the instrument are selected by the musician, the carpenter shapes the inner canal. The brassware maker moulds the *'pyala'* according to the size of the instrument.

They make the pipe too that is known as the *'nali'*. Now, an experienced *shehnai* player makes the seven holes according to the requirements.

It is believed that an old carpenter, Master Shafi Khan of Kolia Bazar, in Benaras, who used to make *'hookah'*, was the main *shehnai* maker in India. After his death, his able daughter took over the profession. She now makes exquisite and delicate instruments for the *shehnai*-players.

As far as Bismillah Khan is concerned, the master himself makes the instrument, and so does his able disciple Jagdish.

5

The Sun Rises

BISMILLAH KHAN

The year was 1916, time, just after *Holi*. The Spring was at its prime in Dumraon, a small princely state in Bihar. With birds crooning and bees buzzing, mother nature was blooming. The forests were colourful, and air fragrant. Every soul was leaping with joy, after the eerie days of the Winter. Pure and innocent life was burgeoning out of the drowsy branches, and decadent swales of yesterday. The whole world had come alive with throbbing activities as the cold atrophy of the frosty winter days could no longer tarry in the warm and sprightly sunshine of the Spring. It was still misty in Dumraon, on 21st March, in the morning. A cool dawn was slowly sending her shimmery shafts of light earthwards. Sleep was reticently departing from the dreamy eyes, blinking in the thinning darkness.

But there was something more in the air today. A kind of new ecstasy. The wind felt softer, the bird-song more melodious. What was it that was making the morning so special? The whole ether was reverberating with a strange, murmuring music. Surely the sun-rise that day had brought some blissful message with it.

Though it was just the wee hour of dawn, yet every soul in the house of Rasool Bux Khan, the *shehnai-nawaz* of the King's court in Bhojpur, Dumraon, in the Shahabad district of Bihar, was up. The father, the elder Khan, and the son Paigambar Bux were getting ready to go to the Prince's palace where they would be playing *shehnai* in the Bihari temple at the morning session of playing. Suddenly, the mother of Paigambar Bux came looking anxious, and asked Rasool Bux not to go to the temple that morning, since Mitthan, the wife of Paigambar Bux was having her labour pain. And so, the old man did not go that morning for the usual rituals. The old lady returned panting with joy after a short while and exclaimed as Paigambar Bux's wife had given birth to an elegant looking boy writhing in her throes. "Congratulations! A little grand-son has arrived for you!" The grand-father remembered God as he uttered "Bismillah". Thus the child was later called as Bismillah Khan although the child's parents named him as Qamruddin in order to have a rhyming with the name of their first born, Shamsuddin, who later became Bismillah's beloved brother and companion.

No one knew on that glistening Spring morning of 21st March, 1916 what destiny had in store for the new born baby. No one could comprehend that a new sun had risen in the sky of Indian music that day with the regular everyday sunrise. A baby sun that was to reach the divine heights of tune and melody with the help of an insignificant and simple instrument called the *shehnai*, in the course of time.

The little baby boy grew up, suckling, weeping and playing like all other babies in the world. Slowly, he learned to crawl on all fours and mumbled innocent words in Arabic and Urdu. Some times baby Bismillah would steal silently unnoticed by his mother near the pools and pond where the shy weeds of *narkat* grew. Somehow he loved the weeds that swayed in the wind with their hollow reeds bending, as though nodding with joy and gratitude at the affection of the child towards them.

Narkat is a special kind of weed that grows in Dumraon over the banks of the river Sone, near the pools, lakes and ponds. The hollow reeds of *narkat* are used in making the pipes of *hookah,* and also they are used at the end of the pipe of the *shehnai* by the *shehnai* players at the place where they blow with their lips to produce the beautiful notes. As baby Bismillah would reach the weeds of *narkat* and touch them with his innocent hands, the trembling, weeds would get over-joyed. Swinging and tangling, they would as though whisper among themselves, "The days of our humiliation will be over now. No more of this melancholy, aloof existence, will be for us. See, the saviour has arrived. He will get us our due position of repute and rank. We will go places now." The mute intuition of the gleeful reeds of *narkat* was to come true as Bismillah grew up to become the Wizard of *shehnai.*

BABY BISMILLAH

At the age of three Bismillah's mother took him and his brother Shamsuddin to their maternal uncle's house in Benaras to celebrate Id. His maternal uncles, like his father, grand-father and all other paternal ancestors were great *shehnai* players. There at his maternal uncles' house the young Bismillah would watch his chhote Mamu, the younger uncle, Ali Bux play and practice *shehnai.* He would no rhythmically at the tunes of his *Mamu's shehnai* and listen intently. The little child's reactions to his music astonished his uncle, Ustad Ali Bux, and he predicted to his sister, Bismillah's mother, that the boy was going to become a reputable *shehnai* player one day.

As Bismillah grew up in the house of his maternal uncles, he became more and more fond of music and musical instruments, especially the *shehnai.* The whole ambience of the house was woven in music, rhythm and tune. At the right-hand side of the corridor in the house was the room where his elder maternal uncle Vilayat Hussain, fondly called Vilayatu, would play his *shehnai.* He was a master of *tan* and *laya,* the intricate articulation of melodies. Bismillah's *Chhote Mamu*, who was to become his teacher later, practiced in the left-hand side room. As a young boy Bismillah did not like his studies. He would rather sneak out while others toiled with their books and play marble in the corridor listening to the enticing music of *shehnai* coming out of the rooms of his *Mamus*. He would hit his marbles the moment a *'Sam'* would arrive as his uncles practiced. He played even his marbles in tune.

Early in the morning, Ali Bux would go to the Jadau or Vishnu temple of Varanasi. He played *shehnai* in this temple every morning, noon, evening and night at a fee of 4 rupees per month. A lucrative sum in those days. Ali Bux will play *Lalit* or *Jogia* with the rising sun and little Bismillah who used to accompany him to the temple would listen to his music dazed and intoxicated.

After playing for the morning session in the Jadau temple, Ali Bux would walk towards the Balaji temple with his young companion, his nephew. A room was reserved in the Balaji temple for the *shehnai-nawaz*. Everyday he would practice there for 4-5 hours. He would come to his senses some time around 11 or 11.30 a.m. to find the little boy watching him and listening to his music all the time remaining hungry. Never ever during his *Mamu's* 4-5 hours practice would young Bismillah disturb him for his own hunger. The *Mamu* would get concerned for his nephew's health and say, "Oh! You must be very hungry! Come let's go home." Thus the pair would return home after their morning rituals and have their meals.

Little Bismillah often wondered as to why his *Mamu* every day went to the room in the Balaji temple for his practice. He could easily take his exercises and recitations in his own room at home; but he seemed to prefer the room in the temple to that one at home. He was unable to suppress his curiosity after some days and inquired of his uncle, "Why do you go to that room in the Balaji temple for practice when you can very well do it at home? Is there anything special?" The *Mamu* stroked his beautiful locks of hair and answered: "You will learn it one day." "But, *Mamu,* when will I start playing *shehnai*?" asked Bismillah, "Why talk about when; you are going to start today." declared his resolute *Mamu.* And Bismillah's rigorous training started from that portentous day. He would be instructed to practice for half an hour during his early days of tutelage. Later on the duration increased to six hours a day. His *Ustad,* Ali Bux was an exacting teacher, a hard task-master and soon young Bismillah realised that the sonorous flow of luscious music that flowed out of his Mamu's *shehnai,* the gentle and gliding streams of melody like the eternal flow of Ganges, was not so easy to be reproduced. More often than not his own instrument would bring out funny notes which would rather be erroneous. He failed to follow his *Mamu* easily. He laboured through a very methodical training. He would carry on his *riaz* while his *Mamu* would be away. Sometimes a family member walking past his room would hear his wanton tunes and laugh mocking at his inept blowing on the *shehnai.* Bismillah would persevere with his exercises in a more forceful manner with greater strenuous effort aggrieved. But criticism would never be able to deter him, rather he would forge ahead towards the cervitude of his destiny with inspired power of will.

After practising for some days at home he felt that the atmosphere at home was not much suitable for his meditative exercises. He decided to leave home and go to the same room in the Balaji temple where his uncle, his *Ustad* Ali Bux practiced for hours. He asked his *Ustad* for his permission. Even at his tender age Bismillah could discern that his teacher's expressions changed from serene to agitated. Forthwith his *Mamu* darted the arrows of his authoritative questions, "Why,

What's wrong in this house? Why can't you practice here? And yes, tell me, have you prepared your lessons that I gave you yesterday?" The obedient young student yielded to his master's query and repeated his lessons that he had practiced previously with all earnestness. He reproduced his every note with rapt attention, not missing a single phrase lest he should not be granted the permission to practice in the Balaji temple. Around the evening Bismillah's teacher called him. He took him to the Jadaun temple, a temple of Vishnu donated by the Maharaja of Gwalior.

After the *sandhyarati* when the evening recital of *shehnai* was complete, *Ustad* came down from the *naubatkhana*. He took Bismillah to the room in the Balaji temple where he was practicing for the past 18 years. Finally, the teacher had granted the permission to the student.

It was a strange kind of joy that the little boy Bismillah felt as he succeeded to get his teacher's approval. He began to practice in the room of the temple daily. He would practice for 4-6 hours. Inside the room that he would keep bolted, alone with just himself and his beloved music, the young faithful student would thus feel secure and safe. He would go on practicing unmindful of the world, fathoming various heights and depths of the melodies. Almost a year passed and he himself started realising the qualitative difference in his music. After finishing the *'palta'* which is the usual *riaz*, as he would pick up a *'raga'* he would enjoy it thoroughly. Sweeping through the various modes and moodes of *'raga'* he used to get totally engrossed in his music. Nothing really disturbed him. Nothing could divert him from his assiduous path of perseverance. He proved himself to be a perfect student at a tender age, completely worthy of learning. He missed his evening games with his friends; he missed the snacks and cakes that his mother would give him off and on the home and he missed many other pleasures of life that he could have been able to enjoy had he not been practising in the temple room like a recluse from the world. This was the devotion of the student towards his master and his work, this was the iron will, which fetched the rewards from the higher worlds for the disciple. And the young Bismillah Khan had all the ingredients of becoming a true learner. He imbibed the codes of the *guru shishya parampara* by learning them by his heart. With a sorrowful heart he says today that such obedience, such devotion is not seen in the students of the modern era. "One has to efface himself" he states, "then and then only the *assar* (the divine union) occurs. Otherwise you will just have the *kala* (art), but no *'assar'*. Without being humble, without humility, the real learning does not take place."

Almost a year had passed. Practicing on his slender instrument for some time he could now feel, as though he was swimming through the waves of his own music. Closing his eyes he would get entirely absorbed in the mellifluous tunes of his melody.

One day during his morning *talim* (training) he disclosed to his *Mamu* how he felt when he did his evening *riaz*. *Mamu* looked directly in his eyes and told "Whatever be the state of your mind while you are playing, keep it to yourself. Not only that if ever you see or feel anything while practising, keep that too to yourself. Don't tell anyone." Bismillah did not understand a thing, whatever his teacher told him. He stared him with innocent eyes. "Don't look at me like a fool. Don't even tell me anything. Do you understand?" The Guru instructed the neophyte. But did Bismillah really understand anything in his childish amazement? Although he nodded like an obedient student, he neither understood nor paid any serious attention.

The summer came, and Bismillah went to Dumraon, in Bihar, to visit his father and grand-father. He was very proud of the skill that he had picked up. He was impatient to show it to his grand- father who was a well-known *shehnai-nawaz*. As Bismillah played on his instrument his grand-father roared in his lion's voice, "Bismille, Bismille." The startled boy came running and said, "Yes sir." The old *shehnai-nawaz,* knowing the potential of the boy uttered in the same booming voice of his, "What are you doing here sirring me? Don't you know, you belong to a family of great *shehnai* players. Don't miaow, roar like a lion. You are a man after all, not a woman. Don't you think, you should play like a man?" Bismillah was puzzled. The rupee his grand-father gave him in appreciation of his recital just a while ago, got wet in his sweating fist. What was his grand-father talking about? He had thought that he liked his music as he had given him a rupee. Why then was he contradicting himself? The grand-mother came out from indoors waving her fingers and nagging. "Why are you after the boy? Let him be in peace. We do not want another *shehnai* player in the family. What do you get, you who are proud of being *shehnai-nawajs*? You are called to initiate every auspicious occasion at people's houses, but do they let you enter their houses even now as most of you *shehnai* players in India have changed your religion and have become Muslims? You still belong to the lower and untouchable castes as before. You are still the Dharkars, Chamars and Doms for the higher castes in the Hindu community. Aren't you say? You still have to sit on the *verandah* at the entrance of a house while playing! The *naabatkhanas* are always outside the premises of the houses! And what do they give you to sit on? *Tats*, hassocks, and cushions made of sacks? Ah! What reputation! Do you call this honour? To hell with such honour! Let the boy do some business. Let him learn some craft which will be useful. At least he will be able to earn his living" taunted the agrieved woman. "Don't you talk in matters you don't understand. Just shut up and go back to your work," the grand-father commanded. His wife's criticisms failed completely to make him doubt the worth of his art and skill. He was proud as before to be a well-known *shehnai-nawaz*. The old man picked up the instrument of the little boy and blew it. And what a sound came out of the instrument: Bismillah could hardly believe that it was his own instrument. It was like the bursting of thunder, like water gushing out of a narrow escape with tremendous force. The volume and the strength of the very first note brought down the whole house in shambles. How could his grand-father play another's instrument with such command, and distinctive technique of controlling the breath? The young Bismillah was electrified. He resolved to learn the secret of this stupendous volume and power. He decided to improve his breathing. As grand-father stopped his grand music, he said to Bismillah, "no health, no breath, no music."

Bismillah had learnt a great lesson. He pondered on it, determined to blend the sonorous quality of sweet tuning of *Mamu* with the strength and command of grand-father's volume. But how to do it? Bismillah was sad. He contemplated more and tried to understand how to become energetic as his grand-father. He decided to give up all whims and caprices that he would show while eating. He became serious about his food habits. The days of eating the extra bites at the affectionate requests of his mother and *Nani* (the maternal grand-mother) were gone. He started exercising regularly. He would drink a big glass of milk, and chew some *badams* (nuts) in the morning and run a long distance. Within seven days during the vacation in Dumraon, Bismillah noticed the change in the tonal quality of his music as his breathing improved considerably. He could breath breathe deeper now and could retain his breath for a long time. The instrument had its own limitations too. It had only seven holes covering only half or a quarter of its length. Thus it could bring out only a limited range of notes, as Khan Sahib explains today.

6

Spiritual Blessings

Once Bismillah went back to Benaras, he started listening to his elder *Mamu* with greater interest. This *Mamu* was an expert in *layakari* and *tan*. He began to fuse the mastery of the three great musicians in his own *shehnai*, the clear and voluminous stamina and strength of his grandpa, the intricate technique of his elder *Mamu*, and the lilting mellifluous peculiarity of his *Ustad*. His music gradually transformed into a *sangam* (confluence) of three unique characteristics of *shehnai* playing. Locking himself in the room of the Balaji temple his *sadhna* (deep meditation) prospered to reach out the melodies of the spheres. Yes, now he could listen to his music and reveal, slowly bathing in the *sangam* of his elder's flow of music. But what was it? Who are they standing round him? He felt that he was getting influenced by his grand-father and his elder *Mamu*. "It must not be like that! I must stick to my *Ustad* alone, otherwise I would be betraying him. I can't do that!" Apprehensive of his own tendencies, the student stopped playing and opened eyes. A beautiful pair of feet, not just fair, almost pink were before his down-cast-eyes. Who was it? Who was in the room? Whose feet were they? Totally taken by surprise Bismillah slowly raised his quivery eyes. There he was. Six feet or more tall, clad in a saffron robe standing before him with a stick in his right hand and a `*commandal*' (a round copper or brass flask of water with a snout and nozzle which the Yogis or sages carry in their hands; they keep the holy water in it) in his left hand. With a beaming face the holy man gestured him to carry on and said, "Play, play." But how could Bismillah play any more! He was so scared. His whole body was numbed in awe. A spell of silence fell as he constantly stared at the man's smiling unearthly face with his frightened eyes. Finally, the man gave a big and hearty laugh saying, *"Mazaa karega, mazaa karega"*. (You will produce bliss). Bismillah's little body shook at the thundering notes of the saffron clad man's laughter. He blinked and then the man was no more before him. How strange! How could anyone disappear like that? He wanted to have the holy man's blessings. *"Baba, Baba,"* little Bismillah shouted. The door was bolted from inside as before. He opened the door and ran out. No one could climb down so far. The *ghat* was two hundred steps away. But there was no sign of the strange man anywhere. Oh God! Why didn't he play his music for him? Was it the experience that *Mamu* was talking about the other day? As the spell of awe and quivering was over, Bismillah collected himself, and picked up his instrument. "I must tell *Mamu* about the incident," he thought, and ran down the stairs. A couple of steps and he was home.

Pale in fear, with his body still trembling in ecstasy he reached his *Mamu* as he ran out of his breath. *"Mamu, Mamu"*, Bismillah could hardly speak. His *Mamu* did not look at him. He talked and continued giving instructions to others. The young boy could not wait, he must tell him. He was afraid of his *Ustad*, but somehow he mustered courage, and poured out the whole incident. He had barely finished when he had a complete blackout before his eyes. His *Mamu* had given a hard slap on his cheek. "Didn't I tell you not to tell even me anything? You idiot! You little ass!" his *Ustad* exclaimed in his rage. "You have lost it. You have lost it", lamented the teacher, "Can't you hold back anything? You worthless fool!" *Mamu* cried out again being sad of his student's ignorance. "I have been warning you since long. Where does the *Ustad* come in between you and whom you saw? It's a private affair for everybody, did I not tell you. You want to become a musician, you, who fails to suppress even a breath? Gone, gone, you missed the opportunity! Will never get it again!" he repeated.

Every prophesy of Bismillah's *Ustad* had come true, excepting this. His spiritual experiences continued for the next three and a half years, but Bismillah had taken a firm resolution. He never made the mistake of divulging the secrets to anyone again. Not even to his beloved *Ustad*. But the blessings of these spiritual happenings and the supernatural visitants have remained with him till date, rather they have increased in a certain sense. The maestro, who lives the life of a detached *fakir* today in his maternal ancestors' house in Sarai Harra locality of Benia Bagh, in Benaras, discloses describing his feelings and experiences that while he plays before the audience sometimes he forgets where he is sitting. It seems to him as though he is playing in a *mazar* (a grave of a Muslim *fakir*), or before the ancient sages and saints. Sometimes he would feel that it is not he who is playing the *shehnai*. As if some other power has got the control the instrument. The world famous *shehnai-nawaz* declares that while the audience bestows him the accolades outside, with closed eyes, he seeks the commendations of his teachers inside, and he becomes satisfied only when he feels that his teachers are appreciating him. These show that although he is acclaimed world- wide today, yet he has remained the student of the yesteryears in his secret heart. He still longs for the pattings of his venerated teachers, and reaches unknown worlds of blessings as he weaves the tunes of his marvelous music. Yes, he has the *'assar'*, the impact in his music that flows from his devout discipleship and his union with the higher spheres of music.

I remember of going through the same kind of trauma after

I lost my two teachers, Siddheshwari Devi and Begum Akhtar. Once I went to Bismillah Khan Sahib to take an interview. He was under the impression that I was a student of Begum Akhtar alone. He did not know that I went back to my teacher Siddheswari Devi again after Begum Akhtar's death. Khan Sahib was intrigued, and asked how it had happened. I told him the story. The story goes as follows:

It was the early Spring-time in February, 1975. The award-giving ceremony of the distinguished *sitar*-player Nikhil Banerjee was going on in the Sangeet Natak Academy, on the specially erected stage at Rabindra Bhavan. As the eminent sitarist came on the stage to play his instrument, I became happy, since Shree Nikhil Banerjee was well known to me because of my long association with him. The *alaap* in *'vilambit'* of the sitarist was so good that I did not want to hear the rest of his rendition. I sneaked out of the hall, and sat outside on the peon's stool. Destiny is a strange thing, and I hardly knew what destiny had in store for me on that day.

I kept on sitting over the stool in the semi-darkness for some-time. Suddenly, I saw Shardaji stealing silently away from the programme hall. Ms. Sharda Rao, an eminent citizen of Delhi, was in the ministry of education during the days when Humaun Kabir was the minister of education. I was surprised to see Shardaji sneaking out like that. I enquired as to why she was leaving the function in the middle like that. She said, "It is important, please don't tell anyone. I have to go. A great saint has come here. I would have to go and see him." Although, I did not believe in such spiritual leaders, I asked Shardaji, if I could accompany her to her destination as I was sitting idle. I told her clearly that I would not go to meet that saint, but sit outside in the car. Shardaji agreed, and destiny smiled at my naive unconcern.

As her destination arrived, Shardaji went inside the building where the saint was staying. I sat in the car according to the agreement between us. Time passed, and it started getting late. I was getting impatient, sitting alone inside the car. After waiting for quite a long time, I decided to go inside the building, and fetch Shardaji. A little away from the entrance there was a long stair-case. Each step of the stair-case was crowded with innumerable pairs of shoes, sandals and slippers. I met people as I climbed the flights of stairs. Each one of them directed me upwards saying, "*Upar, upar.*" I went on climbing, to reach at the end of the stairs, where there was a hall. As I reached the hall I saw that some film was going on inside. I was almost dazzled by the beauty of a comely and serene face soon as I entered the place. There was a kind of halo round the lovely visage which I saw and the face itself shone with a strange, lightful aura. Entranced, I walked towards the magnificently glowing face. It beckoned to me in the dusky hall like a radiant star. Oblivious of the whole ambience, I walked towards the shining image, as I saw an affectionate gesture. He was the saint. He was beaming at me. He was calling me near him. I reached, completely unaware of the other people's presence in the hall.

There were musical instruments beside him. I was given a *tanpura* and was invited to sing. Without a second thought, I started singing like a person in a trance the *raga Yaman*.

It was excellent music that I sang that day. My own voice and technique surprised me. I wondered if it was I or some other mysterious master-voice singing. I stopped singing, but was still overwhelmed by the grand presence of the holy soul. He was constantly smiling, and I knew he liked my music. But he did not say anything. There was a slate near him on which he wrote in Hindi, "*Kutch maango*" (Ask for something). Suddenly, I was able to regain my defiant trend of the mind at this point, and mockingly said to him, "I don't need anything, but even if I want something, you must know it!" He made two tickmarks over the slate which meant `Correct'. A voice in the twilight declared, "Baba is saying that your music was excellent. It has made him very happy."

I became aware at once of the presence of the other people in the hall. I spotted Shardaji sitting among the throng. The hall was full of faces. I got flustered since so long I have been thinking my self to be alone at that place. Suddenly, a quite familiar voice cried out from among the crowd, "She is the girl, *Baba*, she is the girl, Swamiji. She has betrayed me so badly. She was my student, but now she has joined someone else. The item that she has now presented before you is also mine. She had learnt it from me." I was alarmed. I recognized her. She was Siddheswari Devi, my teacher, who tied the `*ganda*' on my wrist. I did not notice her sitting near-by in the multitude. I had gone to learn from Begum Akhtar with her consent, but now she was unhappy about the whole affair. She rushed towards my bewitching angel, and started complaining. The holy man listened to her patiently, as my teacher wept profusely and talked. He asked me at the end, "Can you come to Haridwar with me on the ocassion of the Shivaratri?" A loud clamour rose in the crowd as soon as the saint uttered these words. People shouted saying, "*Baba*, this is not fair. We are your followers. We have been coming to you since very long. Besides, she is not even a disciple. How can she go with you? Why are you depriving us from such a favour?" An utter chaos developed within a few moments. I saw Shardaji nodding approvingly at *Baba*. She was saying, "Why not *Baba*! She will definitely go. I will take her. Thus, I too will get a chance to be near you on the occasion of Shivaratri." I found myself giving my consent without thinking over the matter twice.

Shivaratri came, and I went to Haridwar with Baba and his group. Once we reached Haridwar *Baba* said that we will have bath eight or *prahars*. He asked us to join him for the baths in the holy Ganges. Everybody was happy to join him. I too went with the party. Most people, as we reached the *ghat* plunged into the water of the sacred river. I being ignorant of the art of swimming, remained at the *ghat*, sprinkling a little water here and there on my body, and thus finishing my holy bath. *Baba*, the divine man, entered the water as soon as we reached the *ghat*. He was an excellent swimmer. His white limbs and radiant face floating and swaying in the water made a most beautiful scene. He was a very handsome man with a supple body and tall stature. I watched him playing with the water like a sparkling white whale from the bank. His attraction for me was peculiar and hypnotic.

Suddenly, one of *Baba's* disciple, who was also skimming through the undulating water with the Baba, came near the *ghat*. He shouted, "Baba is calling Siddheswari Devi and Rita Ganguly. They must reach him." My teacher, Siddheswari Devi, jumped into the water with her big and bulky body as soon as she heard at the summon. There was a loud thumping noise over the water and she sailed through the water splashing powerfully. I knew she would reach the Guru, but what about me? I was a black-sheep in that game. Hurdled by my inexperience, I silently watched my teacher swim deftly. Suddenly, my empty eyes spotted the disciple of the holy man again. He was coming towards the *ghat* over anew. He shouted at me, "*Baba* says that you climb down the steps of the *ghat* clutching on to the chain. Stop going down as soon as you find no more steps under your feet. That much will do." I did not know what to do. I looked at the steps of the *ghat* and the chain, without being able to understand if I should proceed on the way that I was directed. There was Shardaji and many other followers of the *Baba* on the *ghat*. They advised me not to worry and do as Baba had asked me to do. "*Baba* is with you.

Don't be afraid. Hold the chain, and go down. Nothing bad will happen." Said all of them. Still secretly dreading the water in my heart, I went towards the steps of the *ghat*. Clasping the chain tightly in my hands I slowly climbed down, and stopped soon as I found no more steps under my feet. I met the holy saint and my teacher Siddheswari Devi there. The *Baba* said to my teacher, "She is your true disciple. Tie a *ganda* on her wrist again and teach eight *ragas* in eight hours to her. Do not worry any longer. Everything will be alright." As we reached the *ghat* after the Baba instructed us like this, I heard people calling out at me, "We did not know that you were such a good liar! You are such a fantastic swimmer, and you told us that you did not know how to swim?" What was all that? I could scarcely understand what people were saying. How could that have been possible? I swam? I had already told them that I had no knowledge of that skill. What are they blaming me for then? I never left the last step under the water of the *ghat*! I never let the chain go out of my frightened grip, and they were claiming that they saw me swimming proficiently! I was sure, they were not telling the truth. But then how could so many people lie together? Yet what they were saying could never be true, because I never knew how to swim! The whole incident baffled me. Siddheshwari Devi tied a *ganda* on my wrist again, and I learned eight *ragas* in eight hours from her. I became her disciple anew as Baba had suggested, but I failed to comprehend the strange happening. I can not swim till today, and do not surmise yet how could so many people see me swimming that day when I did not have even the elementary knowledge of swimming!

I told Khan Sahib about the strange incident, as we discussed about seeing and knowing supernatural things while going on the path of musical *sadhna*. I told him how the whole happening had intrigued and awed me. He looked at me with a serious gaze in his bright eyes, and said, "No, don't ever tell about these things to anyone. I warn you, like my *Ustad* had warned me." I remained silent before his great experience and venerable aura. In a way Khan Sahib was my teacher too. Once during my earlier meetings with him, he advised me, "Practice one thing, one *bandish*, one strain, everyday, unfailingly at the same time. This is essential to become a true musician, to get the `*assar*' in your music." I follow his advice till date. And so, how could I contradict him when he warned me, and advised not to tell anything about my supersensible experiences?

7

Adolescent Days

The child grew up to become an adolescent. The typical phase had arrived in Bismillah's life when he began to get intrigued by the fair-sex. He became fond of bioscope, especially of the enchanting sirens of the silver screen of the silent era.

His favourite actresses were Sulochana and Madhuri. Sulochana was the great heart-throb of the silent era of movies who created a big sensation at that time by giving a 10 minute-long kissing scene in a film. It is the longest kiss ever given on the tinsel screen by any woman. (It was for that sensuous scene which the actress gave the necessity of a censor-board was felt, and created by the authorities in India). Sulochana's appearance on the screen was greeted with applause and showers of money. The great singer of Benaras gharana, Mahadev Mishra relates that the young boy, Bismillah, would be lying on the seats at the front row of the theatre, playing his favourite flute. Perhaps he would be serenading the charming Sulochana to appear soon on the screen or who knows may be he would be keeping seats for his friends who were yet to come by stretching over the seats! Mahadev Mishra, who was a famous singer, in his hauteur, would order Bismillah, "Hey Bismillah, *aage chal, aage chal* (go ahead, leave the seats)." The famed singer did not know at that time that the young and insignificant boy would get honour to the city of Benaras one day by playing his magical *shehnai* all over the world.

Going to the cinema was an important affair for Bismillah at that time. He had grown up into a handsome and well-groomed lad. Dressed smartly with collyrium in his large eyes, twinkling with mischief, he would enter the theatre with his thickly pomaded, curly hair. After all, seeing Sulochana on the screen was not a simple matter! Khan Sahib remembers the beauty of the enchantress Sulochana till today. Describing her attraction he says that her *"amad"* (entrance) would put the crowd in a trance. He remembers the long ordeal of collecting the *`annas'* from his elders for the films. He used to start with his *Ustad* and then would go to the elder *Mamu,* finally seeking the help of his grand-mother for the balance. He would suffer the pain of standing in the long queues for the tickets. The arrival of Sulochana's films would be publicised by big painted banners mounted on *tongas.* The cast and highlights of the film would be announced over microphone. The young lad would run after the *tonga* with the crowd, screaming and collecting the flying hand-bills. He would have a colossal task ahead of finishing his *riaz* properly and perfectly so that he could extract a *`bakshish'* (reward) from his Ustad of at least an *`anna'*. He knew he would be able to do that by his flawless recital of the lessons. Standing in the queue for the movie ticket after arranging for all the money also used to be a monstrous task. Bismillah would think he had won a war as he would emerge out of the pushing, shouting and thronging crowd with his ticket in his hand. With his clothes all crushed and crumpled, his smart locks of hair disheveleed, he would look quite exhausted. He would go home, change his clothes, preen his plumes, and then come back to the theater, ready to watch his favourite film. At the interval Bismillah would leave the theater selling his ticket at half the price. The next day he would come again fashionably dressed during the interval, buy a ticket at a lesser price than the one he obtained yesterday by selling his own ticket. He would enter the theater again, and see the rest of the movie. What thrift! What economy! One can find this thrift, this economy in Khan Sahib's music also. He will never repeat a phrase, a nuance unless it is necessary.

THE INFLUENCE OF THE AMBIENCE

Benia Bagh is a small locality in Benaras. It is inhabited mostly by the Moslems. It is a place where the petty shop keepers and artisans live. They produce Benaras's acclaimed handicrafts. On one side of Sarai Harra in Benia bagh where Bismillah's house is situated is Narial Bazzar. The great nightingale of Indian classical music, Vidyadhari, lived here. Other famed musicians lived in Machhera Bazar, on the other side of Sarai Harra. My teacher, Siddheshwari Devi, the Thumri queen of Benaras lived at the beginning of the Chowk. In order to reach the Balaji temple Bismillah had to pass through a narrow lane called Dalmandi, the famous place of Benaras that was fraught with the fascinating sounds of music all the way. The well-known professional singing women stayed here, in that lane. They performed throughout the night the exqisite melodies of our yesteryears. It was the time when practically all the celebrated *tabla* and *sarangi* players of Benaras would accompany the *mujra,* the songs and dances of the women artists. It was a time of glory and grandeour for the Benaras *gharana*. The colour and spirit of classical music and dance soared to their peaks during this era. There was no TV and cinema. These women were the means of communication, and they were the master entertainers to the music lovers. It was the time of the World War I when black money had begun to flow into the market. Business and commerce was acquiring new dimensions. A group of new-fangled, keen listeners of music arose during this period. Equipped with their new-gained money, they achieved the access to the circles of aristocracy. Listening to good classical music no longer remained the prerogatives of the royalties. All the well- known singers of Benaras by this time had acquired chambers in the narrow lane of Dalmandi. There was stiff competition among these song-birds. Each one of them was a brilliant singer in her own right, and everyone was at the prime of her career. The curse of microphone had not reached yet the music rooms, and so every singer worked hard to make her voice audible from a great distance. The superb exposition of the *ragas* by these excellent musicians of Dalmandi, as they entertained their patrons, with their immaculate *'murki'*, *'khatka'*, and *'zamzana'* through *'kahan'* (articulation) with the correct emphasis of dialect glided from note to note spinning a musical spectrum. After every five yards one could hear splendid and winning melodies of these performing artists in this narrow lane.

Everyday after his *riaz* in the Balaji temple, young Bismillah would invariably have a stop-over below the *'kotha'* of Rasoolan and Batoolan. The two musical sisters would be singing a *'chhota khayal'* in *'Puria Kalyan'*. With eyes closed the young lad will listen to the song, imbibing every depth and height of the tunes with rapt attention. Leaning on the walls of the staircase which took the listeners upstairs to Rasoolan's chamber he would follow the myriad meanderings of the *'khayal'*, and music-borne he would reach the lightful realms of glee. Once the item was finished the *sarangi* started tuning its strings to *'maddham gram'* (C major)- the husky, golden voice of Rasoolan now began a *thumri*:

"Jaag padi mein to pia ke jagaye"

(My beloved woke me up and I was aroused)

The deft singer wove a new musical pattern with each and every word-phrase. With closed eyes Bismillah harkened again. He saw distinctly in front of him the *nayika* in pain. With a deep sigh he would move on to the next canopy where Vidyadhari would be singing the *raga Behag*.

The gliding notes of *ni, pa* in her exquisite style of rendering opened a new horizon of *'meend'* before young Bismillah. And through the little lilt of *ga, ma, ga, sa* that led to a flirtatious landing in *sa* unveiled the mystery of the *raga*. Bismillah could actually visualise the beauty of *Behag*. What Vidyadhari felt was of no concern to the youth, but his personal realization as a student was important. He learnt how to present a composition of *raga* in a straightforward and yet effective manner.

As the rendering of *Behag* drew to a close with a big *tehai*, Bismillah was compelled to praise the excellent striking on the *tabla*, the flawless beats like the rumblings of thunder. It was Kanthe Maharaj playing the *tabla*. Oh! What a fine *tabla* accompaniment to have! Now she started a *thumri* in *Gaur Sarang*:

"Bainya na gaho..."

(Do not hold and twist my wrists)

The voice of the singer would bring out the *'ched chhad'* (teasing), the naughtiness of the beloved making the maiden restless and embarrassed. But then who is teasing the beautiful maiden? With closed eyes Bismillah tried to know. A kind of duality that he had never felt before, crept in his mind. He found the same kind of good feelings in Vidyadhari's song which he felt after prayers and *dua*. The unseen *balma* (beloved) in the singer's music, had some connection with his *khuda*, his Allah, his God. But then what was he thinking? It was *gunah*, it was sin. He should refrain from thinking like that. But why should he stop thinking like that? The sound of music which gave him such joy and peace, could not be a *gunah*, could not be a sin! Something was wrong somewhere? His faith in Allah deepened somehow with his flight through the scintilating notes of the music, yet doubt filtered through his mind. He could not trust the man-made ways, rituals and codes. Agitated, he travelled another five yards.

Five yards more, and the swift *'tan'* (notes) of *Adana* in a high-pitched voice strained through his ears. Bismillah was enthralled. Who was it singing with such expertise? Each syllable was coming out like pearls of Basra. Was it Mushtari? No doubt it was she, Bismillah was able to discern the owner of the fantastic voice, as she sang on the difficult strains:

"E ri mohe jane de, dheet langarva..."

(Let me go, you obstinate beloved)

It was an extension of the same mood that Vidyadhari was singing. Hence it was *thumri.* She brought out an undercurrent of pathos, though the text and the *nayika* were apparently same; there was a clear and unmistakable difference. Was it the *raga* that was making the difference, or was it the melody structure or was it the person rendering? While listening to Mushtari, Bismillah got the conscious *talim* (training) of *Nayiakabhed* and *Avasthabhed.* It was the *mugdha-nayika* here, the young maiden, unlike earlier one in Vidyadhari's song, a *pragya-nayika* - the experienced heroine. May be that was why the undercurrent of pathos. Bismillah moved on further, and stopped beneath the eaves of Rajeshwari.

Accompanied by her daughter Kamla, Rajeshwari was presenting *dadra* in *raga Piloo* to her entranced listeners:

"Sanvaria pyara re more guinya..."

(O my comely, handsome beloved)

Gopal Mishra accompanying her with his famous *sarangi* filled the recital with fast bowing on the instrument with his exact technique.

The young Bismillah reached the threshold of Moti Bai's portal now. The instruments of the *tabla* accompanist with her produced enormous and vivid sounds of thunders clapping, and streams cascading down the mountain peaks. It was the great Nokhelal (later known as Anokhe Lal, a name given by

Pt. Onkar Nath. He said that Nokhe Lal was actually Anokhe Lal, *i.e.,* unique) of Benaras. At the tail end of the *thumri* piece Moti Bai sang:

"Hum se na bolo Raja

Piraye mori ankhia..."

(Do not speak to me my lord, my eyes are aching. I have been waiting for you all the night...)

Nokhe Lal's exquisite *'laggi'*, carried Bismillah's heart to a different realm of ecstasy.

As the song would end with the line:

"Bhor bhaye ghar aaye Sainya..."

(My beloved came home in the morning)

A totally engrossed Bismillah would start with a jolt. He was getting terribly late. He should have gone home by this time; but then his soul was still thirsty for more music, his heart was still yearning, there is one more place to go. He arrived at the gate of the *thumri* Queen, Siddheshwari Devi's house at the Chowk.

The *thumri* expert Siddheshwari Devi was rendering Radhika's jealousy for the flute of Krishna in her *thumri.* Radhika was astonished as to why her beloved Krishna was so fond of his flute which was nothing but a bamboo pipe. Bismillah swayed in the perfect tunes of the golden voice as she sang:

"Muralia kaun guman bhai

na sone ki, no roope ki..."

(O flute why are you so proud neither are you made of gold, nor of silver...)

Just then the young listener of the song-birds got a pinch at his stomach. "So then the great fun is here? Going to the *kothas* right at this age? People at home must be worried by this time!" It was Shamsuddin, who chided his brother. "But then there is nothing wrong in listening to such great and noble music!" Though Bismillah was embarrassed he tried to save his face.

"Shut up," Shamsuddin scolded again as the younger brother tried to argue and explain the cause of his delay. "Everything is great here. Don't tell at home where I caught you. You are too young to understand this place," his brother advised Bismillah. "Of course not, I am a big man now." "Bismillah was indignant at his brother's statement. Way back home, hardly a *furlong* had they crossed and Bismillah reproduced all the strains and `*bandishes*' he heard that day, humming all over again. Soon as he would reach home, he would go up-stairs, in his room at the third floor, close the door and start playing all the tunes with his *shehnai*. He would often repeat this routine after coming back from his *riaz*.

A musical phrase or a '*bandish*' once heard has remained with him till date. And thus unwitting, the renowned song-birds of Benaras nurtured an extraordinary talent by singing love's want and fulfilment in their unmatched *thumris, dadras* and *khayals*.

Once I went to interview Khan Sahib while working on my project over the professional singing women. He, in his fal-setto voice immaculately sang out each and every '*bandish*' of the *gayaki* of the yesterera.

JOURNEY BEGINS

Bismillah was going on 14 years. 1930, *Chhote Mamu* had begun his packing. He was to leave for the Allahabad Music Conference. It was an important assignment where many an eminent musician were to come. Bismillah's *Ustad* was to start the evening with his auspicious *shehnai* music. Young Bismillah was in tears. He was deeply attached to his teacher. He was getting hiccups, and it seemed that the boy would not survive without his master. The winter afternoon presaged something and finally *Mamu* changed his mind. He took Bismillah along with him in the car that came to fetch him for the function.

Allahabad enjoyed a high profile of sophistication at that time. Ali Bux started the evening with the *'alaap'* of *raga Kedar*. The *'bandish'* that he began after 15 minutes of *'alap'* was a rare piece:

sa sa ma

sa sa pa

sa sa sa

It was an unusual composition that Bismillah's *Mamu* started playing. He stopped looking at his able nephew, and nodded him to play while he was cleaning his fret. It was the first time the young student was hearing his teacher contriving the *'bandish'*. He followed his master and reproduced the composition. Bismillah's notes were flawless, but the bars were different which brought out a new dimension of the unique *'bandish'*. There came a '*Wah, Wah,*" from the audience in spontaneous appreciation. The listener bestowing the accolades was no less than the *Aftabe Mausiqui* - the Sun of music, Ustad Faiyaz Khan. Normally, the great a musicians of those days did not consider *shehnai* as an important instrument, and generally great musicians of Ustad Faiyaz Khan's calibre would not stay till the end of the performance with such patience he showed that evening. At the end of the recital Khan Sahib climbed up the dais. He congratulated Ali Bux for his brilliant performance, and patting Bismillah's back he said to his uncle, "*Massha-allah, ise sambhalke rakhiega, Iske shehnai se kahan ki khushbu aati hai*" (Oh God! Keep this guarded. The music of his *shehnai* gives the flavour of verbal articulation). Eyeing young Bismillah he said, "Work hard and you shall make it." The appreciation from this great musician inspired Bismillah to listen to the other *Ustads* with greater interest. Thus, very consciously, young Bismillah came out of the first phase of training and stepped into the realm of matured music. It was an era of great musicians who regaled their audiences through out the country. In his later life whenever Bismillah would get a chance he made it a point to listen to Ustad Abdul Karim Khan, especially his *Bhairavi*. He is still an ardent admirer of Abdul Karim Khan, his sonorous music which has a spiritual complexion in it. His feminine voice was ideally suited for the *Nayika Bhedh* - the soul lamenting to unite with the Supreme being. His *shehnai* mainly simulates Abdul Karim Khan's voice today.

Khan Sahib's marvelous attachment to Ustad Adbul Karim Khan's music had tied him with the *Ustad* with an invisible bond. Once he was participating in a function on the occasion of Abdul Karim Khan's 'Death Anniversary'. His turn came at 6 o'clock in the morning. Ustad Bismillah Khan tried to start *Todi*, but somehow he began to play *Malkonsh*. Ustad Abdul Karim Khan's disciples who were related to the *Kirana gharana* were present in the audience. Bismillah Khan felt that Abdul Karim Khan was also sitting amidst the crowd. His eyes became moist with tears, as he enjoyed the magical tunes that he himself produced. After a pause he tried to play it again but such magic in the notes did not come. He knew that the departed soul of Ustad Adbul Karim Khan came to acknowledge Khan Sahib's respect and admiration for him and only then Khan Sahib's realized that he was playing a mid-night *raga* in the morning oblivious of what he was doing. But did, he, himself do it? He only intended to play *Todi*, then have did he start playing *Malkonsh*? Many of the disciples of Abdul Karim Khan, who were present there, remember the morning of Bismillah's, recital and describe the recital as an unique experience, since they could hear Abdul Karim Khan coming alive through Bismillah Khan's *shehnai* on that morning.

As a boy he was deeply influenced by the powerful voice of Ustad Faiyaz Khan, particularly by his *'pukar'* and *'meend'*. He used to get swayed by his renderings.

Bismillah was also magnetized by Pt. Onkar Nath, chiefly his *desi Todi.* Haphiz Ali Khan's *Darbari,* Enayat Khan and his rendering of *Jai Javanti* were the other sources of enrichment for Bismillah. Khan Sahib still cherishes the memories of these delightful days.

A new chapter, according to Khan Sahib, an insignificant one, started in his life, with his marriage to his elder *Mamu's* daughter, in 1932. A cousin, whom he frequently met at home, and might have played with, suddenly acquired the right of sharing his bed. It was a decision made by the elders. Bismillah had no part in the decision, nor had he any choice. He was not to analyse the implications of the new happening in his life. He was only to obey the verdict.

It is a custom in Muslim marriages that the groom looks into a large mirror, which is kept in between the bride and the groom and thus both of them get the first glimpse of their faces. Bismillah felt a chill in his spine. He trembled, and felt shy but then the bride's eyes met his own embarrassed gaze and he knew the truth.

Bespangled in her silk, brocade and embroideries of gold, she was neither Sulochana, nor Madhuri, the silver-screen sirens whom Bismillah admired. A simple girl with mundane thoughts, she had no great tastes and understanding for music. At the tender age of 16, Bismillah did not understand much about the intimate relationships in the conjugal life, the burden that he was to bear for the rest of the life. Strangely enough, every time I asked a question about her, Khan Sahib would invariably change the topic. He does not want to discuss about the 50 years of long life that he has shared with the only one woman, in his life. He refuses to let anyone encroach upon his memory of the first experience of the opposite sex.

Khan Sahib has proved himself to be a faithful husband, never faltering. The only temptation that he reluctantly recollects came when a sort of romance developed with a very beautiful maiden from an affluent background. Under the pretext of going to Ajmer Sharif, a plan was chalked out between them, which could have been an affair of intense passion. On the way to Benaras the woman died in a crash. With a deep sigh Khan Sahib today recollects the tragedy and thanks Allah for saving him from committing a *gunah* (a sin). Never again in his long life has he slipped. Women of every clan and strata have followed him in the country and abroad, but no amount of allurement could turn him into a pleasure seeker. Unwavering, he is carrying on the relationship with the only woman he has known in his life, giving her the gift of nine children. The bond that his elders tied him to, he is blamelessly keeping its honour.

He still remembers that his *Ustad* said if one goes for pleasure- seeking, music would be lost. Khan Sahib is still the same obedient student of his wise *Ustad*, and following his guru's words. He is not attached to anything in the world. Neither his children, nor the glitters of the modern society attract him. A saint at heart, and a mystic by temperament Bismillah Khan, who reached the world of the Supreme Spirit through his music at the age of six has no other romance of flesh and blood in his life except his unique, singular romance with his divine music. Be it erotic or sublime love, he has conjured everything up into a single whole in the form of his music. Hence Bismillah Khan and his matchless melodies enjoy a pure and holy union with the spirit. A peculiar oneness that occurs when one gives everything the whole of oneself, all emotions, passions and love to his music, and music alone. It becomes a great love, an unparalleled romance. A kind of romance we rarely find in other musicians who scatter their energies in weaving thoughts other than the dreams of their music.

THE MUTUAL ADMIRATION BETWEEN COLLEAGUES

It was a night after his marriage, and Khan Sahib was lying on the bed beside his wife. It was a quiet night and a cool, pleasant east wind was blowing. Suddenly, the strains of a unique music filled his ears. The maestro could not recognise the voice at first. He thought a *farishta*, an angel from heaven must be singing somewhere. Slowly, after a while, he was able to comprehend the words, and the voice that was singing. It was the impeccable voice of the then Akhtari Bai Faizabadi who later became Begum Akhtar (my teacher). She was singing her famous *'ghazal'* in *raga Jogia Bhairavi*:

"Deewana bana na hai to de..."

(Make me crazy... if you wish...)

Someone was playing the song on a record-player. Khan Sahib was struck by the notes of the song. He sat up, erect on his bed, unable to sleep and started smoking a cigarette. The song glided through the still of the night like a bird softly floating in the cloud-less blue. Puffing his cigarette, his only addiction in life, Khan Sahib listened to the intoxicating music totally revealing in the expanding weft of the notes. "*Wah! Wah! Wah! Wah!*," he constantly praised the excellent music. Completely unable to understand his happiness, his wife asked, "What are you doing *Wah-Wahing* in the dead of the night?" Aggravated by her tasteless query, Khan Sahib said to his wife, "Don't speak now. Go to sleep. What will you understand of this exquisite melody! You ignorant woman! Don't talk and disturb me, otherwise I will go somewhere down-stairs." His wife, his better half, was insensitive to the ecstasy that sweet tunes of the *ghazal* gave him in the quiet of the night. They were as though dwellers of two different worlds. She did not understand the mysterious romance of her husband with music. The next day Khan Sahib went to the record company looking for the record of the song that he heard the night before. He bought the record, and listened to it getting absorbed in the delirious melody over and over again.

During early 70s, *Ammi* (my teacher, Begum Akhtar) came to Delhi. She called me up from hotel Nirula, where she liked to stay. As I reached the hotel she asked me to find out the phone number of Rajdhani hotel. She knew that Ustad Bismillah Khan was staying in that hotel. As I got the number she started talking to Khan Sahib in a friendly manner constantly giggling and teasing. I was able to gather from the conversation that she had with Khan Sahib, she promised a meeting somewhere that evening.

In the evening, I went with Ammi, to Naina Devi, the well-known singer's house, in Vinay Marg. Naina Devi was the disciple of Rasoolan Bai. She was married in the royal family of Kapurthala. We were ushered in a spacious room at Naina Devi's residence. There were pictures in silver frames declaring the affluence of the royal family. After a while Khan Sahib came out of a room. He had come to Delhi to perform with Naina Devi in a programme. As Naina Devi and Khan Sahib practised, my teacher Begum Akhtar exclaimed, "How could she venture to do such difficult thing? Singing with you is a more than formidable job! Khan Sahib with his characteristic humility replied, "*Badi bhali aurat hai.* (She is a good woman)." He had no qualms about playing with a singer who could not match his pitch. Ustad Bismillah Khan's *thumri,* is *thumri* par excellence. Even Begum Akhtar, who was a master of *thumri* herself, never ventured to sing with him. She would say, "Why should I show such audacity? He is the master. No one can match his pitch. Why should I loose my respect knowingly, performing with the master, who makes words and articulations with no words and literature, just by playing his instrument with his intricate technique?" At the end of their practice that day Khan Sahib said to Naina Devi in his curious modest tone, "I will keep my pitch low tomorrow. It will be convenient for you." I was surprised at his amazing unselfish approach, his lack of pride.

While returning to her hotel *Ammi* became quite upset. She told me angrily, *"Tum atai log baaz nahin aoge."* (You non-professionals will never learn). I could understand the cause of her displeasure. *Ammi* was a staunch admirer of Khan Sahib. She did not like the repetition of a combination of a note before reaching the `*nyas*' in a swift frequency, which is a peculiarity of the Banaras *ang* music. She would say, *"Sui fans gai." i.e.,* the needle has got stuck. She admired Khan Sahib, as he did not do any repetitions. She would often say, "Learn from him. He has taken what is good in a style, and has discarded what is unimportant." There was a strange mutual admiration between Begum Akhtar and Khan Sahib. The harmonious chord vibrating between them was almost tangible.

In the second All India Music Conference that Bismillah attended with his *Ustad* Ali Bux, he was adulated again. He received a gold medal this time. In 1937, Bismillah again enchanted his listeners with the mastery of his music in the All India Music Conference. His brother, Shamsuddin accompanied him on that occasion. This time he was given three gold medals. Khan Sahib still proudly speaks about them. He earned his national fame from this conference. But according to Khan Sahib, it was with his performance on the 16th of April 1938, on the occasion of the opening of the All India Radio Lucknow, his growth in status as an artist began. Without any feeling of shame he describes how he practised in a garage-like dwelling place of a friend before he gave that particular performance.

A new venue of performance opened for Bismillah Khan through the A.I.R. But the days of happiness were not to be for long. Bismillah Khan received tremendous shock with the death of his *Mamu,* his beloved *Ustad,* in 1940. It was the first death in the family. A pall of sorrow hovered over the family with the departure of Ali Bux. Bismillah was unable to accept this separation with his teacher. He wept and wept ceaselessly. Day and night his eyes would never be dry. Who was going to play the beautiful tunes for him now? He felt lonely. One day Bismillah tried to play a tune that his *Mamu* would often hum when he was alive. It was a piece sung by Ustad Bade Ghulam Ali Khan. *Mamu* used to be a great fan of Ghulam Ali. Khan Sahib says that this Ustad was an exceptional singer. No one would think that it was not Bade Ghulam Ali singing when Ali Bux would sing in his own voice. Such was the resemblance of the two voices. As Bismillah tried to play the tune, he failed to reproduce it. With a broken heart he retired to bed. Sleep overpowered his sorrow-laden eyes quickly. While asleep he saw a dream of *Mamu.* He rebuked Bismillah in the dream for not being able to reproduce the tune, and instructed his beloved student how to go about the tune. Bismillah felt ashamed of his weakness as he woke up. He endeavored again, and as he says, "*Baat ban gai.*" (It was accomplished) He reproduced the tune perfectly. Such is the attachment of the student with his master. It is an immortal bond. The *Guru* and the *Shishya* are inseparable forever.

8

Sadhana

It was time when the movement for independence was becoming intense. Every woman performing artist would start their evening programmes with an invocation to the mother-land. Fight for freedom was in the air. With that movement for freedom in the country, another conflict, a struggle for liberty, franchise emerged in the heart of Bismillah Khan. He started realizing the claustrophobic situation of the *shehnai* players in the country. They were allowed to play only at the periphery position. He soon understood that it was not true that without *shehnai,* festivals would not start. The entire concept was off-key somewhere. Why was it that a *shehnai*-player was not welcomed in a house? Why was that it in a '*dangal*', where two professional musicians get into a duel, the *shehnai*-players are never included? Not only they are never permitted to take part in a '*dangal*', they are given just hassocks to sit on, spread outside the court-yards while playing in a social function. Now, if the great leaders of the country were fighting to free the mother-land from the shackles of the British, Bismillah Khan as a servant of *Saraswati* must free his instrument, the *shehnai,* from that terrible fate of playing in a procession, walking on the street, getting a second grade position in the hierarchy of the musicians. His hard work doubled, so did he increase the intensity of his prayers. *Dua,* his sincere prayers alone would change the fate of his instrument. He now meticulously incorporated all the high-brow technical manoeuvrings that a wizard of music would employ through his stringed instrument. He took in the entire gamut of the contrivances and techniques of classical music, like, *'lari'*, *'jod'* and *'jhhala'* in his music. He introduced all the cunnings and crafts in the tones of his *shehnai*. The memory of Ustad Alauddin Khan's music enriched his *riaz*, and in the treatment of *ragas* he had the blessings of *ustad* Faiyaz Khan. Bismillah's music embraced the *'laykari'*, *'tehai'*, and *'pukar'*, all the flourishes of Ustad Faiyaz Khan. He could now weave the iridescence of the rainbow with his microtonal accuracy. He developed endless repertoire with his diligence, and arduous practice. He produced enchanting melody with effortless improvisation. His communication through his music became pure and perfect, influenced by the art and skill of the professional-singing women, whose spirited music he was able to imbibe as a child, Bismillah Khan's music was integrated now, completely equipped, the virtuoso now earned the venerable name, Khan Sahib. His great virtuosity fetched him rank and position in the music world. His amazing skill made him the wizard of *shehnai* for the rest of the world. Bismillah Khan and his *shehnai* gained admiration in the nation and abroad. Along with his recognition the country also saw the days of independence on the 15th of August, 1947. Bismillah Khan became the first free Indian to address the nation even before India's first Prime Minister, Pt. Nehru could come to the microphone to greet the people, early morning on the auspicious occasion of the Independence day. He congratulated the whole country with his transcendent charisma of music while Mahtma Gandhi, Rafi Ahmad Kidwai, Maulana Abdul Kalam Azad, Sardar Ballabhbhai Patel, and other stalwarts of the struggle for Independence sat in the audience. Finally, the days of bondage, disgrace and frustration were over. The *shehnai* and the *shehnai* player had established their long deserved significance in the realm of classical music of the free India.

After *Mamu* passed away, Shamsuddin started looking after the home-front and Bismillah went for the programmes, but destiny had another blow to offer Bismillah. Shamsuddin also departed leaving Bismillah alone to keep alight the candles of the Benaras *gharana* in 1951.

With the untimely death of Shamsuddin, Bismillah's attraction for the material world ended, although there was no looking back in his career of music. One after another award, and honour came on his way, but he accepted them with a marked detachment. Nothing could touch this musical *yogi* of Benaras. His children, his fame, his wealth, everything was insignificant for him, save his music. His curious tunes of *shehnai* that tied him with his *Ustad*, his beloved brother and great ancestors.

In 1936 Khan Sahib received the Sangeet Natak Akademi Award. The President's awards came one after the other: the Padmashri in 1961, Padma Bhushan in 1968 and in 1980 the Padam Vibhushan. He received the Doctor of Letters from the Benaras Hindu University in the same year. Vishwabharati honoured the noble doyen of *shehnai* with the Deshikottama award.

The detachment, the unfastened attitude of mind, became conspicuous in Bismillah Khan's character after his brother's sad death. But it was not new in him. He had been detached during his childhood too when he played a recluse to the world confining himself in the secluded room of the Balaji temple for hours, living his life through the flowing notes of his music alone. If one carefully looks at the photograph in which Bismillah Khan stands among the great gaints of the classical music-world of the yester era, he will find the characteristic detachment over the face and posture of Bismillah

Khan. Even when he stands among an amalgamation of stars where everybody was supposed to stand close together due to lack of space, Bismillah maintains his peculiar aloofness. No wonder that such a man will be disinterested in the pomp and show of the modern, contemporary world of media. What does he care for a book being written on him? We can not capture his music nor can we capture the rainbows of his personality! He is totally indifferent about what media has to offer him. Of fame, he has no dearth. He has ample money too. He supports almost a hundred kith and kin with his money. Nothing binds him, except his love for music. He loves the city of Lord Shiva, Benaras, where his favourite river Ganges flows weaving everlasting melodies day and night. He loves playing on the *ghats* of the holy river at night. He rests here in peace with his great musical romance. Once an American Business tycoon wished to create a second Benaras in the U.S.A. for Khan Sahib. His *shehnai* had bewitched the rich man, but Khan Sahib refused the offer. How could he leave the place where he fell in love with the only romance he has in his life, his spiritual music? How could he abandon the beloved banks of river Ganges for the charm and allurement of an alien land? His peace is here where he finds the divine oneness with his precious music. His music that he produces blowing through the hollow reeds of *narkat,* kept hidden at the blowing end of the pipe of the *shehnai*. The dreams and intuitions of the hollow reeds of *narkat* in Dumraon have come true. Bismillah has led them to honour from disgrace. The child of Dumraon has conquered the world with the tunes of his *shehnai*.

Bismillah Khan's *shehnai* can make one weep and smile simultaneously. Once when Maharaja of Dumraon called him to Clark Hotel in the scorching heat of the month of June, Khan Sahib said that it would rain as he would play. And it really rained to the surprise of the obstinate heat waves of the summer in Benaras. His teacher Ali Bux could light up *divas* and candles with his music and could make the rain fall (as Khan Sahib says). Bismillah Khan is a worthy student of his *Ustad*. His music can actually create miracles.

If I am asked why on the earth did I choose to write something on Bismillah Khan, to my mind he is the true symbol of contemporary secularism. With the death of Vidyadhari, Badi Moti Bai, Chhoti Moti Bai, Rasoolan, Batoolan, the *thumri* queen Siddheshwari Devi and the other prominent singers of Benaras, the golden era of Benaras *gharana* music concluded. With the death of Begum Akhtar, the radiant star of classical music, the Lucknow *gharana* of music, was finished. Only in Khan Sahib Bismillah Khan's music I find my teachers the late Siddheshwari Devi and Begum Akhtar ocassionally alive.

India has been condemned throughout the world for casteism, communalism and other negative practices. All these issues are relevant. But the people we are discussing here could express themselves freely without ever getting touched by the hell-flames of negative attitude or prejudices. The people of India have given them a place in their hearts. They have honoured without failing the magic and magnificence of the art, the healing power of music.

Indian people have been second to none to pay respect where the respect is due. Mahatma Gandhi is recognised as the greatest Brahmin here, the embodiment of knowledge and humanity. So is it with Bismillah Khan. Khan Sahib and his music is beyond all castes and creeds. It has a special place of honour in the heart of the common man as have the hereditary musicians of *dhadi, mirasi* or *gandharva-katthak* community. Thus to me his recognition in the society is the ideal example of secularism in our caste and community ridden society.

A TRUE MUSLIM

Khan Sahib says that as good and true music takes you to

the domain of the Supreme being, so do all true religions. It is the same place where every yearning soul looks for peace. He is a devout *shia* Muslim, who never misses his *namaz*. He prays five times a day regularly. Music is *haraam* (taboo) for Muslims, but for Bismillah Khan without any traces of qualms music is divine, his *shehnai* is his Quran.

He says, "How could my music that gives me such peace and happiness be *haraam*? I reach the light of my Allah with the waves of my tunes. I am searching the ultimate Truth travelling through the resonance of my music, and you call it *haraam*?" What belligerance? The *shia* maulvis fall silent before his innocent reasoning. Every year, on the eighth day of Muharram this defiant *shia* Muslim leads a procession through the narrow and dingy lanes of Benaras, proudly displaying his rebellion by blowing on his *shehnai*. A special *shehnai* made of silver is kept for this religious ocassion. He will lead the mass expressing his emotional exuberance through his music, and reach the *rawzaa* of the martyr Imam Hussain. Sitting cross-legged like a forlorn pauper on the dusty ground, this great minstrel of music will play for hours weeping incessantly, while the crowd will throw coins at this white clad symbol of devotion. His music is his life, his only religion, one can understand on that day.

I wonder who is a Muslim, in the true sense of the word? After all Khan Sahib believes in one and only God, Allah. He salutes *Nabi* (the prophet); he observes 30 days of *roza*. According to Islamic preaching he gives alms, the right percentage of his earnings during this period. He does not touch liquer nor eat pork; he is not promiscuous, if there is anything that he hates, it is alcohol. As a musician he observes Muharram unfailingly. How many Muslims today can boast of all these virtues before they challenge Bismillah Khan's music as a *gunah*? When such a devout Muslim claims 'music' as divine, how could that music be called *haraam*? Afterall, no Muslim in the world can deny that Hazrat Bilal had a sonorous and musical voice, and the Rasool himself would get inspired by the *'azaan'* that he gave in his luscious voice!

Any human being who has the discipline of not missing his *'namaz'* for the past 70 years, his expression through his music automatically reaches a height-the miracle of *Sadhna*. The Annual Music Festival organised by the great Sitar maestro Pt. Ravi Shankar was once attended by all the stalwarts of the music world. Starting from the evening each musician unfolded the magic of the important *ragas* of that time (a Indian melodic structure strictly observes the time cycle). Though it was usualy unlikely, yet the young sarod-maestro, Ustad Amjad Ali Khan found himself performing at the tail-end. The morning was almost approaching. As a torch-bearer of a great gharana, young Amjad had the enormous task of keeping prestige before the giants of the music world. Evidently, he was nervous. He realised that he must surrender to his *Ustad*. He closed his eyes and started playing *'Latitdhvani'*, a *raga* that he himself had composed, employing two *'maddhamas'*, *'shuddha'* and *'teebra'*. His surrender to his *Ustad* was duly rewarded. Amjad continued. His *'sachha sur'* (true music) prevented Khan Sahib from going for his *'namaz'*, although it was time for his *'namaz'*. He sat back and listened to the music of Amjad Ali. Later he commented that Saraswati was flowing out of Amjad's music. Such a music was as good as *'namaz'*. The employment of two *'maddhamas'* made the rendering holy, as *'namaz'*. He never fails to appreciate the young musicians with his whole heart whenever he gets a chance to do that. A quality of character rarely found in the great musicians of his rank and calibre.

Birju Maharaj, the doyen of Indian classical dance relates about his luck of receiving the blessed affection and love of Ustad Bismillah Khan. Khan Sahib is the contemporary of the

Kathak maestro's father Achhan Maharaj and famous uncle, the master of *Kathak*, the great Shambhu Maharaj (my teacher). Being the youngest in the family, the Kathak doyen was the most loved child in the family, and so whenever and wherever Khan Sahib meets him, be it in a concert or during a journey together, he will invariably embrace Maharajji. The *Ustad* will bless him fondly and give him *'dua'*. The *Kathak* maestro recounts that both he and Khan Sahib would be very happy to find each other in a concert. "He is always an inspiration to me whenever I find him in a concert or in the audience," says Birju Maharaj. Once Khan Sahib said to him, *"Shambhu ne mujhhe bhav batakar rulaya, tere naatch men kya hai, mujhhe rulaya?"* (Shambhu made me weep with by his *bhav* (expression), but what do you have in your dance that made me weep?) The *Kathak* adept says, "I was overwhelmed by that comment of Khan Sahib. It was great commendation for me. To hear something like that from an artist of such grand calibre and experience is something really moving." I remembered the time when I used to learn *bhav* from Shambhu Maharaj. It was from him, for the first time, I got a glimpse of the world of *thumri*, so vast and exquisite. It was during his class, Siddheshwari Devi heard me, and decided to teach me as her first *'gandabandh' shagird* (disciple). The incident was like this that Siddheshwari Devi sang and Shambhu Maharaj gave *bhav*. Both of them were in tears, and I, watching them, literally started crying with hiccups. While Siddheshwari Devi patted me, Shambhu Maharaj, who had an inept sense of humour, said, "The music of Benaras makes every body weep. This is a strange quality of Banaras *ang*." He laughed and added, *"Banaras men Ganga to bahati hai naa, isiliye yeh Banaras ang sabki akhon se Ganga bahati hai. Amaan Bismillah lakdi chabaike rula deta hai! Kambakht kya bajata hai, kaleja nikalke rakh deta hia."* (Because the Ganges flows in Benaras, the Banaras *ang* makes the same flow of the river Ganges ooze out of every body's eyes. Look at

Bismillah, he makes you weep while he chews a piece of wood. God! How he plays! He takes out your heart!) Birju Maharaj is also influenced by Ustad Bismillah Khan's music deeply like his famous uncle. "Khan Sahib is a source of inspiration, he says, "one should learn from him, from his love and dedication to music. I am on his way. He is a true lover of music, and his love is pious and sacred. I feel lucky enough to get the love of such a saint, such a *fakir* of the music-world." He is lucky, truly fortunate, I thought. He has received the affection of a sage, whose music has solaced the world, and who is not reluctant to show his appreciation to the younger artists.

Birju Maharaj states that one could see the impacts of the *ragas* and *'sur'* over Khan Sahib's face as he plays his *shehnai*. He is not one of those artists who perform with a stony face. Khan Sahib's face, his gestures, and especially his twinkling eyes, reflect the kind of emotions he is expressing through his recital. While performing Ustad Bismillah Khan becomes an epitome of the musical arrangement that he is presenting. And that is an important trait is any artist. This makes the *Ustad* a complete artist. The Kathak doyen described here had Khan Sahib asking the people in his party to share betel nuts with Birju Maharaj once when they went to Russia together, where Birju Maharaj found himself in the want of betel nuts. Khan Sahib like the Kathak maestro is also fond of *paan* (betel leaves), a speciality of Benaras, and the Ustad has no qualms about sharing his things with others.

FIRST JOURNEY BY PLANE

With the coming of Independence in 1947, the patronage of music by aristocracy was displaced by political and middle class patronage. The success of Indian musicians in Europe and America, oddly enough, brought lustre to music at home. The growing middle-class suddenly became aware of India's musical tradition. It became fashionable to attend concerts.

The Union Government accepted Maulana Abdul Kalam Azad's brain-child, and created the Indian Council of Cultural Relations (ICCR). One of Khan Sahib's earliest visits abroad sponsored by ICCR was to Afghanistan. The trip was a big success. King Zair Shah of Afghanistan lauded the performance of the maestro, and showered valuable gifts of priceless Persian carpets and other souvenirs, none of which Khan Sahib possesses now. A fakir that he is, he little cares to stack up worldly commodities. Thus, in his house, there are only two rickety benches to sit on.

In 1965, Khan Sahib was to go for the Edinburgh Festival as well as the Commonwealth Arts Festival. The other conspicuous personalities of the music world to go were Imarat Khan, Vilayat Khan, Pal Ghat Mani Aiyyar, Kishan Maharaj, Shanta Prasad, Pt. Ravi Shankar and Ali Akbar Khan. The delegation was led by Shri K.S. Kothari of the Sangeet Natak Akademi. Khan Sahib agreed only on one condition that he would not mind starting two months ahead of the show, but he would not fly.

It took all the power of persuation of the ICCR officials and well-wishers to coax Khan Sahib to agree to fly at that time. He was frightened to fly like a child. He was not going to sit in an aeroplane, for he was not sure if it would really come down once it goes up. Besides, it was against the will of *Khuda*. Men are not supposed to fly; otherwise he could have had the gift of a pair of wings from Heavens. He understood quite well the flight of the human mind in the realms of dreams and wonders. He was an expert to soar with the tunes of music into the starry worlds of mysteries; but developing actual physical wings was disastrous! Definitely, *Khuda* would not be happy about such a weird thing! Finally, a consent was wheedled out of him with an assurance that he would be allowed to go for a Haj, the most cherished experience for any Muslim in the world. At last, as he sat in the plane, and his seat-belts were being fastened, he started reciting verses from Quran. His throat dried and choked. Mr. Kothary, sitting next to him realized the situation. He asked the air-hostess to give him a glass of juice. Trying to assure him about safety, he said, "Look at these young girls. They are moving about freely. They are not afraid! All these passengers are with you. Nothing will go wrong." Khan Sahib felt a little secure. Just then a voice coming from the microphone ordered the passengers on-board to extinguish their cigarettes. Thy young girls moving around the corridors also went back to their seats. Now, Khan Sahib was alarmed. The girls were fastening their seat-belts. "Bismillah Khan your days are numbered." thought the simple man of Benaras. Everybody looked so serious strapped to their seats. The innocent magician of music closed his eyes. He was getting funny sensations of fear in his solar plexus. Holding his breath he waited for some mishap to take place. But time passed, and nothing happened. Still apprehensive, he opened his eyes. The young air-hostess was again standing before him with a tray of food, and a hot towel to wipe his face. Khan Sahib was drenched in perspiration during the take-off.

Today Ustad Bismillah Khan flies practically every second day all over the world, although he would like to go still by a train, if given a chance, and that too in a second class, where the feel of the common man exists, which is not found in the isolated compartments. Even travelling by a train becomes frightening for the master when he has to journey alone in a closed compartment of Ist class.

Ustad Bismillah Khan achieved the great honour of performing at the Lincon Centre Hall in America. He was the first Indian to get such a unique opportunity. As he faced the vast crowd in the foreign land, he felt a bit uneasy, but then he spotted Vilayat Khan, the great *sitar*-maestro, sitting in the crowd.

The presence of Vilayat Khan in the audience inspired him, and he performed at his best on that occasion. At the end of the programme the audience was so overwhelmed by his music that he had to take seven curtain-calls. On his seventh curtain-call he was given the microphone and requested to say something. By this time Khan Sahib was craving for a cup of tea. He was thirsty. In India, a cup of tea, would have arrived, right on the stage. In the land of white-man everything was strange. He had just then expressed whatever he wanted to express through his instrument. Why did they want him to talk?

The clapping continued in the hall. The crowd intoxicated by his magical performance was noweager to hear his voice. The maestro stood with folded hands on the stage. He preferred *'namaskar'* to *'salaam'* on that occasion. He said, without caring if the people were understanding his language, "Why are you making me run so much? I have toiled so long with my instrument before you. Now what's the fun of making me run?" The crowd burst into laughter, and the noise of the clapping increased. Khan Sahib carried on, in his simple language, "I beg your pardon now. Let me go. I would like to have some tea now." Khan Sahib paused a while then, smiling said again, "In our country there is a proverb that a wise man talks less. So please do not ask me to speak if you have not missed the wisdom of my music." More laughter and clappings filled the hall. Khan Sahib left the stage, and did not return again. The simple man of Benaras did not know how to become proud of his own prowess. No amount of adulation could make him forget his humility. Arrogance could never become his cup of tea. His simplicity and humbleness adorned him perfectly. He went to America for just 2-3 days, but he stayed there one and a half month.

A SYMBOL OF FORTUNE

A golden era in the Indian panorama of films arrived with

the coming of the two superhit films, *'Ramrajya'* and *'Bharatmilap'* based on mythology. These films were made by the well-known Bhatt brothers of the Bombay film industry; Vijay Bhatt and Shankar Bhatt. The famous director Mahesh Bhatt of today's film world also belong to this illustrious Bhatt family of directors. Thus, the contribution of the Bhatt family to the Indian cinema is no less than five decades. After the two immensely successful mythological films the Bhatt brothers brought *'Vaiju Bawra'*- a film made on the life of a great classical singer. The film was a huge success. For the first time, the renowned master-professional- singers agreed to take part in that film. Ustad Ameer Khan sang for Tansen in this film while Mohammad Rafi sang the songs of Baiju. After the splendid film *'Baiju Bawra'* of the Bhatt brothers, another master director Shree V. Shantaram presented his exotic film based on the classical dances of India. The film was unique since never before a film was made with a hero as a classical dancer, as it was in *'Jhhanak Jhhanak Payal Baje'*. The hero was the expert classical dancer Gopi Krishna. As the film made a silver jubilee, V. Shantaram arranged a gala classical music festival in celebration of the success of the film. Top rank professional-musicians were invited to perform in the festival. Ustad Bismillah Khan also performed in that festival. He played *raga Behag*. Vijay Bhatt, who was present in the festival was so impressed by his performance that he began pondering on the idea of making a film not with the usual concept of making the hero sing, instead having the hero play *shehnai*. Thus, came the dream of the famous film *'Gunj Uthi Shehnai'* into being which later was to become a beautiful reality. I am sure, director Vijay Bhatt did not realize at that time that he not only was going to introduce *shehnai* as a classical instrument popularizing it though the film, but was unknowingly going to break the barriers to give status to an instrument that had so far been neglected by the dons of the classical world. Not only that he was to give the social upliftment to *shehnai* with the help of the man who fought relentlessly to get rid of the stigma attached to the *shehnai* and its players, but the film also opened a new horizon, and raised the stiffled voice of the *shehnai* with the tuneful notes played by Ustad Bismillah Khan - the child of Dumraon who fulfilled his promise of bringing grace to the insignificant instrument-*shehnai*.

The film world madly believes in astrology and numerology. Even today the modern cinema world with its advanced technology of photography, sound system and other devices depends on these ancient sciences of the stars. No film starts without having an astrologically calculated time for its inception. Also, the names of the films are frequently based on numerology. Many superhit films have the mystery of their success hidden behind their names which vibrate to the tunes of fortunate numbers. The film *'Gunj Uthi Shehnai'* received a strange vibration which numerologically signifies some change, the coming of something new in the usual arena of life; and the film fulfilled outright what its name implied, since it introduced the *shehnai* as its hero's beloved musical instrument. The astrologers considered the nuances of their mathematics, and the time augured well, making the film a terrific success. Ustad Bismillah Khan remained favourite as he had already become a symbol of good-luck.

The *Ustad* and his group were invited to Bombay. Bismillah gave his consent after a great deal of convincing. At Bombay, to the surprise of the directors and producers, he chose to stay in a small Muslim hotel, at the Victoria Terminus. It was very unlike the other great artists who always prefer to stay in luxury hotels. The budget that was kept for him and his team of ten people remained unutilized.

The *Ustad* liked the music director Shree Vasant Desai, but the scene at recording and the environment were completely alien to him. The studios, big machines, rush and great frequency of flattery, all these gave the master a strange feeling. He felt like an outlander who believed in a slower pace of work. He longed for quietiude, concentration and details. The buzz and bustle of the tinsel town made him sick. Nevertheless, he had already started composing in his mind. A complete transferring of the *shehnai* music was to be done to suit the voice of Lata Mangeshkar. The Producers and directors, unfamiliar with the style of work of Bismillah Khan got alarmed. They were afraid that Khan Sahib might make it a heavy classical piece, not realising that Khan Sahib is probably one of those few masters whose music equally elates a child and a grown-up. He knew the popular need, and understood the mass psychology very well. The producers and directors underestimated their lucky star. Imagining Khan Sahib a novice they started tampering with his work. They started telling the master what made a hit tune. Khan Sahib listened to their ignorant suggestions with a calm face, nodding occasionally, while his eyes twinkled with the familiar mischief. His smile encouraged the producers to become even more enthusiastic about explaining film music. At the end of their dialogue he quietly said, "Yes, I have understood what you want. Please do not worry." He turned round and ordered his party to pack up for Benaras saying, "The Seth know more than us; why are we wasting time here!" There was clear mockery in his voice. That brought the producers on their knees at once. They begged for forgiveness. The song composed by Bismillah Khan and sung by Lata Mangeshkar *'Dil ka khilona hai toot gaya'* turned out to be a big hit. It has not lost its old popularity even today.

The first chunk of recording for the *shehnai* music that was to be implanted in the film was done with *Ustad* Ameer Khan. The situation was, the Ustad, who was a vocalist was teaching his very young *shagird* to imitate his voice. The young disciple was later on to become the hero *i.e.,* Rajendra Kumar - the most sought after superhit hero of the yesteryears. The great master of *shehnai* was so brilliant that he executed the *'taalim'* portion of the disciple, in which the boy had not got much virtuosity also exquisitely. Originally, the music director Vasant Desai planned to have the portion in which the child-hero learned from his teacher done by some ordinary *shehnai* player. There was a *shehnai* player in the name of Shyamlal in the industry. The music director did not want Bismillah Khan to go through the unnecessary situation of reproducing the improvisation that was done by his contemporary fellow musician, Ustad Ameer Khan. But Khan Sahib had other ideas. Both Shri Vijay Bhatt and Shankar Bhatt along with their music director Vasant Desai were over-whelmed when Bismillah Khan demanded that he would play for the child also. He was sure- *"Woh bachhe ka phunk alag kaise hoga, agar bade hokar woh mera phunk hoga?"* (How could the blowing of the child be of a different style, if I blow for him as he grows up?) Khan Sahib was correct. With perfect harmony he did the lesson taking piece with Ameer Khan. While most of the musicians need many rounds of re-cordings to meet the expectations of the music director, the two great master got the perfect results in their first take.

The venue was the Mehboob Studio and the recordist, the greatest name of the yesteryear Shree Kaushik. As Shree Bhatt recalls, it was in the evening, they was supposed to record the musical competition required for the film between *sitar* player and the hero. The portion in sitar was to be played by Ustad Halim Zafar Khan who was very young at that time, but was a wizard of his instrument. Young and handsome, Halim Zafar entered the Mehboob Studio immaculately dressed. Bismillah Khan was already there with his party. With a radiant smile he greeted Halim Zafar, *Assalamalequm! Massahallah kya khubsurat lag rhae hain. Jaisa bajaana aisa hi shaql. Sab Allah ki den hai!"* (Hullo! God how handsome you look! Your face is as beautiful as your playing of the *sitar*. It is all God's gift!) Halim Zafar returned the usual greetings. Smiling he took the compliment, and said just a "Thank You" in reply. Director Vijay Bhatt, who was till then busy in the recording chamber entered the studio. He explained the situation for which the recording was to be done. Halim Zafar started tuning his instrument which normally has a lower pitch than the pitch of a male vocalist. Bismillah interrupted Halim Sahib. The pitch was too low for him. But Halim Zafar seemingly oblivious of the maestro's concern went on tuning. After some time, he was ready with his instrument which takes a longer time to get tuned. He tuned it to C sharp as usual, but it was not a suitable pitch for a *shehnai* player. A *shehnai* is generally played in D sharp. The lower the pitch, the more the lung power is required to play the base notes. Khan Shaib suggested, *"Hum thoda utarte hain, tum thoda utho."* (I will come down a bit, while you go up a little.) But Halim Zafar declined point-blank to adjust his pitch with Bismillah Khan. He said nothing in words to reject the proposal, but he made no move to increase his pitch. A hush descended in the studio. Everybody present there looked at one another. The situation was slowly becoming grim. No one spoke. Vasant Desai looked distinctly worried. Halim Zafar was happily playing his `*chikari*' the sympathetic strings. Vijay Bhatt was looking at his elder brother. Young Arun, the son of Vijay Bhatt was also present in the studio. Suddenly Khan Sahib broke the spell by giving a big laugh. He said, *"Main tumhe to haath se nikalna hai, hume to phunk bhaarna hai. Theek hai tum jisme shuru karoge hum Insahallah usi men bajate hai."* (young man, you will pluck your instrument with your hands, but I will have to blow on mine. Anyway, wherever you will start, I will play there by God's grace.) Halim Zafar started playing the intricate stroke works which are possible over sitar and other plucked instruments. Halim Zafar Khan is a master of such techniques. It was be no exaggeration if one says that he has made his instrument a slave. Mischeviously he started playing `*jhhala*' a technical area which is not used or required (because it is not possible) in vocal music or wind instruments. But to his greatest of surprise the expert sitar player realized that Khan Sahib could bring out the same complex patterns through his instrument. Not only that Khan Sahib could generate such intricacies a shade better than his own. It was midnight, and the director declared the end of the day's work. Halim Zafar got up, and prostrated before Ustad Bismillah Khan with tears in his eyes.

The last day of the recording was again in Mehboob studio. Khan Sahib was required to play the rest of the solo portion needed for the film. It started raining in the evening, and by the next day morning the whole city of Bombay was practically flooded, as narrated by Shree Arun Bhatt about the incident. Bismillah Khan was to play a *raga* with improvisation. He explained each note that he would play to his accompanists. He was to give signals, and one by one they were to play just that salient note. He distributed each note to different accompanists. He explained that he would either stamp his knee with a hand or nudge with his elbow, right or left, and for the fifth note he would pull out his ankle. He was to give such signals since he himself would be constantly facing the microphone.

Khan Sahib was in great mood. He started playing with fabulous imagination as the recording started. The requirement of his accompanists was specially designed by Bismillah Khan for film music, in order to create the popular tonal balancing. Unfortunately, on the third note he stopped playing, and started screaming in abusive language in rage. Young Arun Bhatt was taken aback. He had never imagined that the grand sophisticated person had another side of his character. For the next ten minutes, he went on calling names to his party members trembling in anger. He put his *shehnai* down. A complete silence fell in the studio. No body spoke, no body dared to move from his position. Slowly Bismillah Khan changed his reed, and picked up his *shehnai*. He blew it, and then started laughing. The darkness drifted away, and the atmosphere become light. The Bhatts took a sign of relief. Trying to justify his anger Khan Sahib, "Our instrument and reeds are accustomed up `*purvaiya*' (the cool and dry east-wind). This place has a damp climate. Even I find it difficult to play my instrument. It is not the fault of my poor kids. It would be difficult for me too to hold a note in this clammy weather." He closed his eyes, and tears trickled down his cheeks. He took his *shehnai*, and asked the accompanists to change the reeds. He adjusted each reed with his own hands. The recording became perfect, as was desired by the Ustad.

By that time Vijay Bhatt became quite friendly with the maestro. Out of curiosity he asked him, why he started weeping after scolding his party-man. The Ustad answered, "You must have been very sad to see the plight of my fellow accompanists when I rebuked them? You would not understand it. In the Indian music world, these abuses become pearls in your later life."

Shree Vijay Bhatt recalled how the Ustad narrated a story of his childhood. Once, when Bismillah Khan was a little boy, Ustad Ameer Khan came to perform in Benaras. Young Bismillah by that time had become quite proficient with his instrument. His teacher Ali Bux asked him to go into the concert, and listen to Ameer Khan. Quite late in the night when Bismillah entered the house, he found his Ustad awake, and waiting for him. He first inquired whether Bismillah appreciated the recital. "What was the *raga*?" asked the *Ustad*. As Bismillah was raving about the recital, the *Ustad* asked him to give account of each note while the singer improvised. Bismillah explained how the great musician improvised around `*gandhar*', `*madhyam*', and the beautiful use of `*dhaivat*', finally ascending to the higher octave `*Sa*'. He was himself getting thrilled while explaining to his *Ustad*, and describing how Ameer Khan reached the climax. Just then a slap came over Bismillah's face like an anti-climax. "You idiot, unscrupulous fellow! Have you no shame?", the Ustad reprimanded. And then in his shrill voice he sang to show how the master must had used the `*pancham*' which was the most important phase of the *raga*. Young Bismillah was aghast. He cried out, "O! Did you also go to the programmes?" Khan Sahib said he now understood how stupid a question it was to ask his Ustad. Coming to the film world Khan Sahib recognized how important it was to know one note which keeps lingering while the new note emerged. It is this area of Indian music which tends naturally to harmonization (which we often mistake as Western concept). He said, "Bhatt Sahib, this is the reason why I asked the accompanists the bring out the notes one by one. It is in order to maintain the lingering quality which a vocalist easily maintains."

The *Ustad* teacher Ali Bux had rightly advised him not to play complicated *raga* whose identity depend on the thin balance of the two great *ragas*. He asked him to play simple and known *ragas* like, *Kedar*, *Behag*, *Bagesh*ri, *Malkonsh*, *Khamaj* etc. He warned him against the temptation of playing difficult things for getting applauds from the audience and connoisseurs. "Play simple things" Ali Bux told Bismillah, "honestly and sincerely, so that your audience says `*hai ha*i' rather than `*wah wah*', and they exclaim Ah! - instead of `*keya baat hai*' (What mastery!)" While describing all these things Khan Sahib as though realized that he should not waste time in Bombay. Why was he in Bombay now? For money? Or was it fame? Was he looking for a bungalow? Where was his beloved Ganges? Wherc was *Purvaiya*? It was early morning. Throughout the night, it had rained so much that all the roads in Bombay were blocked. There was no chance of moving out of the studio. Drinking tea with a Wills cigarette between his fingers, Khan Sahib saw the sun-rise. He was home-sick. He knew he must return home.

Once, while having a conversation with him I asked Khan Sahib, "What is it that you are asking God to give you for the past 70 years, when you pray?" I could clearly see the change on the face of the religious man which my question had brought about. His eyes, watching some unknown horizons, were lost in a sublime realm of thoughts. "In every" he slowly answered, "that I have made to God, I have asked only one thing, let my music be *ba assar* (immaculate through divine union and harmony)." No wonder that his music brings tears in the eyes, and joy in the hearts of the listeners at the same time. His *shehnai* is dear equally to any kind of audience whether young or old, mystic or debauch, thug or a family man. His room on the third floor of his house in Benia Bagh, is the symbol of Khan Sahib's austerity and modesty. One realizes how true he was when he said that he asked only for *sachha svar* (true music) or *ba assar* music. He neither uses an electric fan, nor any air-conditioner in the scorching heat of the summer in Benaras. He keeps himself cool with the help of a frilled, cane hand-fan, when the heat becomes unbearable. "What about the children, at the end of the *gali* (lane), who have no roof over their heads?" Khan Sahib gives his simple and straight-forward reasons. "I see a young mother at the road-side everyday. She makes a canopy over her new-born baby with a *tat* or any other torn rug, spreading them with the help of four bamboo sticks. She fans her baby to keep it cool in the heat. Thus she fights the cruel summer. How about her?" Who can stop himself from getting touched by the artlessness of this simple argument? Who will venture to ask him more about the cause behind his simple living? He never forgets his bond with the common man. He knows that he is just another human being in the vast human-world. Neither lower, nor higher than anyone here. So what, if he is famous for his fascinating music? Isn't his *ilm*, his genius also given by the same *Khuda*, who had made man? He serves the world with the gift of his enchanting music, and willingly suffers the pains that the common man has to take everyday. This way perhaps he feels close to the fellow humans.

In the winter Khan Sahib would be seen, sitting all by himself, near a small clay oven, with charcoal burning in it, lost in his own thoughts. His room, scantily furnished, also manifests his characteristic simplicity. The bed in the room, but a *charpoy*, with an old bed-sheet spread over it, the sight of such extreme asceticism makes one groan with surprise. It whips with a subtle satire, as one remembers the luxury and lustre amid which today's famous musicians prefer to live. Unlike Khan Sahib, they like to migrate to the huge, and air-conditioned bungalows in the metropolitan cities of the country from their ancestral homes. Here is a man, who still stays in his ancestral house. His plain, simple ways of life but compels one to respect him with a different and deep veneration. He seems to be the real winner in the journey of life. There is no dearth, neither of fame and wealth, nor of humility and simplicity. He still loves to roam through the interweaving lanes of Benia Bagh blowing on his *shehnai*; his inspiration is still where he found his music. This is his strange luxury in life, along with his love for cigarettes, that too of only the Wills brand. He requires nothing more to feel rich and eminent.

If one analyzes Bismillah Khan's music today, one would get the true flavour of Benaras music merged with the revelry of the mellifluous melodies of the *Kirana gharana*, and the clarity of the *Agra gharana*. It is Bismillah Khan who first introduced the *'jod'* and *'jhhala'* - the techniques which are essentially possible to be used in the plucked instruments, in the *shehnai* music. He would produce the same kind of sound as that of playing *jod* and *jhhala*, adding another dimension to his *'gayaki ang'*. The word *gayaki ang* is used for *shehnai* music when the instrumentalist reproduces the exact techniques of a vocal musician. The other *'ang'* being the instrument-technique produced by the two main schools, the technique of the *Veenakar* (one who plays the Veena), and the technique of *Rabab. Jod, jhhala* and *ghasit* have a distinct charm deeply influenced by the natural possibility of these instruments. These techniques are only possible to be generated through the cardeophonic instruments (*tat vadyam*). Bismillah Khan has very intelligently grafted these techniques in his music by manipulating staccato breathing and tongue position. It is not enough just to say that Ustad Bismillah Khan plays through his instrument. Since *shehnai* is a *Sushir Vadya*, and a *Sushir Vadya* is an extension of vocal music. Ustad Bismillah Khan has incorporated that style of vocal music which is actually an area of instrumental music, and has already been explored by the *Senia gharana* maestros by singing *taranas*. What is great about Bismillah Khan is that he has introduced the techniques of the *veenkar* and *rababiya* too in his music, thus giving this instrument a place in the sun. As an ordinary instrument, with hardly one and a half octave range, which had no pedigree whatsoever in the hierarchy of classical instruments of India, *shehnai* has been adorned with rare honour by Ustad Bismillah Khan, by introducing the entire realm of classical music to it. He has brought the refinement of intricate tunes without loosing the rustic quality of the aroma of the earth in the melodies of his *shehnai*. Listening to his music with the eyes closed, gives one the experience of the grand river Ganges gushing out of the foot-hills of the Himalayas, dancing through Varanasi, flowing through Bihar and culminating in the Bay of Bengal. One discerns the delight of the romance through music as Bismillah Khan pours out his whole being through his soulful music.

There are three extraordinary musicians of this century: Ustad Bade Ghulam Ali Khan, Ustad Amir Khan and Ustad Ali Akbar Khan. If one listens to Ustad bade Ghulam Ali, it is aesthetics par excellence, but his music can not be imitated. It is only his hard work, assiduity and aesthetic realisation with which he could create such splendid music which can not be repeated. In the last 50 years, with the emergence of Ustad Amir Khan, one can distinctively see the change in the approach to Indian classical music, since, Ustad Amir Khan brought a new trend of thinking in music. A new path, a new sphere of ecstasy opened before the musicians. Consciously or subconsciously, the music of the *Kirana gharana* has inspired all the contemporary musicians. Ustad Amir Khan reduced the tempo of the *vilambit khayal*, which very intelligently compensated the need of the human psyche to be restful and relaxed in the ambience of the slow exposition. Also there is hardly any instrumentalist in our country today who is not indebted to the great musical philosopher, Ustad Ali Akbar Khan, directly or indirectly. He opened the doors of '*mandra saptak*' and '*taar saptak*' in his *alaap*, thus increasing the entire range of *vilambit* by three fold.

If one listens to these two great musicians, and are not overpowered by their mastery, one can recognize how scrupulously they have used the *vilambit*, the time circle, and turned it into *ati vilambit*. This immense gift from these two celebrated musicians has enabled the modern musicians to impart solace to the restless world of today.

Ustad Bismillah Khan has incorporated the slow exposition of the *Kirana gharana*, and the *Veenkar's* technique of Ustad Ali Akbar Khan in his music, thus opening a third dimension. It is like the opening of the third eye, which is an organ of the soul that does not open easily, and never ever without the proper preparation of hard work and true devotion. His music has become sharp as Shiva's *'trishul'* itself. The musicians today fail to comprehend that like unsealing of the third eye, it is difficult to imitate Ustad Bismillah Khan. He has come to know a new horizon, where one should come equipped with discipline and perseverence, to become a permanent inhabitant.

RECORDS AND CASSETTES

About 15 years ago, I was travelling from Delhi to Madras in the Rajdhani Express. I was going to perform in the Winter festival of Madras. It is delightful initially to sit in an A.C. coach. No pollution, no unpleasant noise. Not even the disturbances of the new platforms approaching, with the hawkers screaming at different pitches, volumes and timbers. But when the night comes near, and one starts feeling sleepy, soon it is realized how important a bed to a human is! Even if you can't sleep or dream, the craving to stretch your legs pesters you, to rest the back somewhere, and lie down a while. Nevertheless, in spite of all hurdles and discomforts, the human being learns to fall asleep automatically due to fatigue. I too must had fallen asleep, otherwise how could I wake up? It was the sound of Ustad Bismillah Khan's *shehnai* that woke me up. He was playing *Jai Jaivanti*, a *raga* that musically pronounces the hour of mid-night. It was a tuneful warning that I will have to bear the trauma of a night without a bed for another couple of hours. But soon, the morning tea, and a sort of break-fast was tossed before me on the table. 'The manager of the train was sensible enough to play Bismillah Khan's *shehnai* in the morning, I thought, only the *raga* was of mid-night. In stead of *Jai Jaivanti*, it should have been Khan Sahib's *Lalit, Bhairavi* or at least *Todi*, the proper *ragas* of the dawn hours. I was forced to get lost in the theory of 'alienation' that we teach at the drama school, while talking about Brecht, the German expressionist dramatist. Eating breakfast with a mid-night *raga*, was a true experience of alienation. That was the only occasion, I remember, I failed to enjoy Khan Sahib's music. But then no, not quite true, it was not with Ustad Bismillah Khan alone, I was vexed by the idea of listening to Bismillah Khan with another musician. It was a *'jugalbandi '*, a duet, and the other musician was V.G. Jog - a marvelous violinist. I can not help recalling my childhood association, whenever I listen to Jog Sahib. his classic moon-like face, fair and hand-some, moves before my eyes. His music even today, to me is an experience of playful joy and mischief. The perfect music pouring out of his violin was disturbed by the soul-wrecking flow of melody of Khan Sahib.

You may have *'sthaibhava'* of *Rati* (Eros), mixed with *'adbhoot'* or *'veer'*, but the ultimate *'rasa'* has to be *'shringara'*. Duality in *'rasa'* experience can be disastrous. I was angry with Khan Sahib. I loved his music from my childhood, and cherished the moments magnetized by his tunes. I could not bear the idea of some alien music disturbing the image that I have of Khan Sahib, although I must admit that I equally admired the alien tunes.

This is another area of Khan Sahib's wondrous personality that I have noticed. While playing with another musician in a *'jugalbandi'*, he never seems to be serious. It is like a pastime, an amusement to him. He frolicks like a little boy who plays a fun-game, in all his *'jugal-bandi'* records. Whether it is with Girija Devi who sings *'chaiti'* and *'kajri'*, the grand maestro of *gayaki-ang sitar* Ustad Vilayat Khan or Pt. V.G. Jog, he never spills his whole-hearted magic of flowing euphony, rather he skips and capers, he restrains his mellow tunes more than revealing his wizardy. He carries on totally oblvious of what the companion has to impart.

In a piece with Ustad Vilayat Khan in *Todi*, he opens his score swaying his impeccable *'shadaj'* over to *'komal gandhar'*. As though with a brush and colour just within that little journey of three notes he paints the rising sun. The Sun, when young Hanuman jumped and captured mistaking it for a ball, created *'anarth'*, i.e. chaos. Exactly in the same way Bismillah Khan at his very first blow conquers *Todi*, resting on *'komal gandhar'*, compelling Vilayat Khan to open his very first passage on *'komal dhaivat'* leaving him no other choice. Occasionally Ustad Vilayat Khan displays his superb mastery over his instrument while dealing with the *raga* in the musical treatment, but Khan Sahib throughout the record plays an immaculate combination of notes with *'meed'*. His awesome command but forces you to take a deep sigh.

In his record with Girija Devi, who also hails from Benaras like Khan Sahib, a repetition of the same trend could be found. Girija Devi starts her *'chaiti'* - *'Chadhala Chait chit na lage Rama'* with a touch of *Jhhinjhhoti*. In spite of the advantage of the literature that she has, the actual *'chit'* (heart), which is restless, manifests itself the moment Khan Sahib repeats the musical arrangement. In his opening piece itself, he establishes the *'virahini nayika'* (the heroine separated from her lover) pining for union while she is staying in her father's house. His *'chit na lage'* takes the listener to the higher realm where the heart begins to long for the union with the Spirit. Thoughout the record, Khan Sahib hardly plays. He seems to be unmindful. This shows that this giant of a musician is least ambitious, and has no scruples about posterity. No wonder that as I told him that I wanted to write his little biography, he was least interested. According to him it is of no use. He says, "What we do here is nothing, but a drop in an ever expanding ocean. We have no separate existence. We are the parts of that great Supreme One. What will remain is music, and once I offer something to the world I dissociate myself from it. I don't try to remember anything any more." True, Bismillah Khan's music that he has offered to solace our trouble torn world has become an entity. It has become a device to reach the domain of peace and unblemished love. There are many musicians today who have learnt to give brilliant interviews as they have become famous, but very few practises what they say. Khan Sahib does. He practise what he preaches.

The only record of *'jugalbandi'* in which Ustad Bismillah Khan has shown the wonders of his technique with exquisite rendering, is with Ustad Halim Zafar Khan, the great *sitar* maestro, who has truly made his instrument, a slave. Both of them played *Kedar*, starting from the very begining the *'drut'* (fast) portion, without pretending any intellectual spell. It is a sheer joy to travel through its technique, speed and *'sachha sur'* (true music).

His performance in the duets except for the one with Ustad Halim Zafar Khan unfolds the curious aloofness of his character. What the other musicians who co-performed with him in the *'jugalbandis'* described were their personal experiences which arose from living full, involved lives. What Bismillah Khan exposed emerged from a life that has detached itself from the tugs and pulls of the mundane world. His life has only one love, only one attraction, his music. Though he never fails to show respect to his co-performers by occasionally pouring out his heart, the true music of Bismillah Khan could be found only when he is playing alone, meditating through his flawless melodies. No other disturbance, no matter how lofty it is can make his music true to itself. Consequently, only in his L.P. recordings we encounter Bismillah Khan in his real colour. His essence leads us to rare ecstatic worlds as we hear him in his L.P. solos. The *Ustad* has no track of his own records, as to have many he has published. A list of his publications is however attached.

Today, the rich and poor both can enjoy the music of the *shehnai* without erecting a *nahabatkhana*. No bookings are needed for the wedding ceremonies. We have become accustomed to Ustad Bismillah Khan's *shehnai* in the atmosphere of festivities. We are so used to the high quality *shehnai* music of Bismillah Khan that now-a-days as we go to some wealthy wedding ceremony, where people can afford to have the *shehnai* players in person, more often than not we are not impressed by the nature and calibre of the music. No wonder, more and more traditional *shehnai* players are taking to flute playing, which has more potentiality, because of the path shown by the great flute player Pannalal Ghosh. One can clearly see the immense resentment among the other *shehnai* players when you mention the name of Bismillah Khan, though they morally can not deny the status that Bismillah Khan has given to the *shehnai*. But at the same time they think that if they would be given a chance like Ustad Bismillah Khan, and the same platform too, they could reach the same height. Few realizes that they would now have to explore new venues as Ustad Bismillah Khan has done as a pioneer. Even his own son, who is playing for thirty years with him, will have to search for new areas, fresh dimensions.

Ever since I have thought of writing a book on Bismillah Khan, I have approached the other *shehnai* players. It is very strange that they have all either contradicted each other on each and every information including the family tree or have avoided talking anything that could be included in the book for reasons best known to them. I am truly grateful to Shri Raghunath Prasanna who whole-heartedly helped me to understand the instrument.

Almighty God must be thanked that Bismillah Khan and his immortal music is living and thriving undaunted in this turbulent world of ours. We can repose in the privacy of our souls with the comfort of his lulling tunes. He is now nearing eighty years of age. He has been richly honoured by the government and the people of his country. He has attained ample degree of material security, and the satisfaction of international recognition. He loves playing in Berlin, Germany, outside the country. In India he likes the crowd of Calcutta and Pune.

In his maternal ancestor's house, in Benia Bagh, Khan Sahib lives with his huge family. His first-born Mehtab Hussain and another son Naiyar Hussain play *shehnai* in the houses of the family clients, like Late Shri Kishori Raman. Another son Kazim Hussain owns a shop in Benaras. Ali Haidar, a son of his brother Late Shamsuddin Khan, is married to his daughter Zarina. He plays *shehnai* in Khan Sahib's party. He loves the first son of his eldest daughter, but the most favourite is Zarina's youngest daughter. She gives him the news of the kitchen, about the special dish that would be cooking there for Khan Sahib. His youngest son Nazim Hussain plays *tabla*. His daughter, Malka Begum, who was married to another son of his brother, Ali Abbas, passed away 5-6 years ago. Bande Ali, son of Akbar Hussain, son of Late Shamsuddin Khan is a graduate, He looks after Khan Sahib's tours abroad.

Previously, Khan Sahib used to play *shehnai*, all through the night regularly, but now-a-days due to health reasons he goes to sleep at 11 o'clock. He loves playing *shehnai* sitting on the Panchganga *ghat* of the river Ganges at night. Every morning, without fail, he wakes up before the sunrise. Without eating anything he spreads the webs of his musical orison to the rising sun in *raga Bhairava*, after completing his regular *namaz*. To the aspiring musicians of today he always says, "Persevere without fail irrespective of whatever mental or bodily condition, you might have. Then one day you will know the secret, and the tunes will roll and frolic at your will." Thus, when you listen to Khan Sahib's music, you tend to believe that pain and ecstasy go hand in hand in his *sadhna*. Although, the mortal body suffers from illness, and the worldly mind pines with the mundane longings, while there are dearths and copiousness in the outer world, the inner being of man yearns and follows an eternal light. The heart, the inner man forges ahead despite of all seeming hurdles after this immortal resplendence.

Inspite of all these, I wondered as I talked to him if it was all truly harmonious without any uneven edge in his life. His simplicity, his perseverence, his own *sadhana* and music, as far as these things are concerned, there are no rough bumps in Khan Sahib's life. He is complete, he is whole in himself. But Khan Sahib seems to be in desperate need of solitude. He does not demand anything, no electricity, no heater nor fan, he just wants to be left alone. He longs to have privacy with his precious music, his means to reach his Allah. One can not help but shudder when one thinks that he is alone responsible for his children, their families including all his grand-children, the daughters of his *Ustad*, their husbands, his brother's children and their families! There are about hundred people for whom the old man of eighty has to provide for. It is a Herculean task, and no matter how much he earns, even if it is a lakh in a month it is not enough. Perhaps this is why Khan Sahib has stopped taking any royalty from his recordings. He takes a lump sum in the beginning instead. Today, he has no track as to how many discs he has. He does not even possess a copies of his own recordings.

As you visit the house of Ustad Bismillah Khan, you become aware that except Khan Sahib with his simple standard of living, the rest of the family is fashionable, and is fond of worldly virtues. I thought, it was a happy experience for Khan Sahib to be surrounded by his people, but I was naive to imagine that. He took a deep sigh as I asked about his brother's children. His eyes were filled with tears, as he narrated many a memorable incident connected with his dear brother. Shamsuddin's death was a shock to him, which he has not been able to overcome till date. All the children of his elder brother are dearer to him than his own children. Most of them are part of his group. Two of his own daughters have been given in marriage-Zarina and Malka, thus making the bondage deeper. Zarina's little-baby-daughter, with whom he is greatly attached, sat on his lap as he talked. But it was not wise of me to ask him about Malka's children. Khan Sahib, evidently wanting to change the topic, started talking about Ustad Abdul Karim Khan, and his treatment of *raga Jogia*. I realized that he wanted to avoid a discussion on the subject which I had rather unadroitly started. Later when I visited Mahadev Mishra, in his house in Rampura, he explained that Ali Abbas, Malka's husband, has been learning form him. No wonder, they say that all that glitters is not gold. Obviously, in spite of Ustad Bismillah Khan's best efforts, the family does not live in all that great harmony. Nevertheless, Malka's children, as a solace, live with Khan Sahib.

DISCIPLE

The *Ustad's* one, and only disciple who joined him as a child like it is in a traditional, *gurukul*. Jagdish Prasad Qamar hails from a simple villager's family. His father Shree Deepchand, was a well-known *nafiri* player in Delhi. He learned from the disciples of Ustad Shadi Ram. Ustad Shadi Ram was a famous *nafiri* player of Delhi. His disciples were Adbul Rahim, Kale Khan, Jagannath and Chhote Mian, who later on prepared many other *nafiri*-players.

Shree Deepchand met Ustad Bismillah Khan, and was immensely influenced by his music. He decided that his son Jagdish must become the disciple of the *shehnai*-maestro and learn the wondrous art of *shehnai*-playing from him. He requested the *Ustad* for his permission. The *Ustad* gave his consent, and Jagdish was sent to Benaras at the tender age of 10 years, in 1946. He was to learn while staying at the master's house.

Now, after 47 years of steady and persistent relationship with his *Ustad*, Jagdishji fondly describes him as a hard-task master and exacting teacher, which the *Ustad's* own teacher, his *Mamu*, Ustad Ali Bux too was. He relates that in the begining Ustad Bismillah Khan gave him just a line phrase of a *'plata'* in *raga 'Bhairo'* to practice, and then as though totally forgot the young Jagdish's presence in his house. We can compare the situation with the childhood of the *Ustad* himself when his *Mamu* would be oblivious of his nephew's presence while practising in the Balaji temple. A self same way of finding out the real desire of the disciple from the heart of his heart was applied by Khan Sahib also. Only perseverance will further the student, only the true love for learning. The student has to pass tough tests in order to prove himself worthy of the knowledge that is to come from the guru. Consequently, Jagdishji, had to go through his chores of waiting with patience and perseverance, until his teacher was satisfied, and started paying him attention.

By and by Jagidsh, the young disciple of Ustad Bismillah Khan became the manager of his house. He earned the trust of his *Ustad*. The *Ustad* would give him the money for the whole month according to the budget, and ask him to run the house with the sum. The thrifty student would obey his teacher's order, but his economy would disturb his *Ustadni* Muggan Khanam. She would demand for more groceries, meat and other goods, saying, "I don't know what goes on between you and your *Ustad*. I have to look after the house. Guests are pouring in day and night. I have to feed them. How shall I do all these things? I do not know where from you get the money for buying the extra goods. I need the things, and that's all." Arguments and counter arguments would gradually grow into a hot discourse between the student and his teacher's wife. The *Ustad* would intervene sometimes and scold the disciple lightly for not obeying his *Ustadni*, and somehow a solution would be found. Jagdishji describes his *Ustadni* as a very affectionate woman. Even though she used to fight with him regularly for the goods and groceries, she never forgot to call Jagdish first, during the meal-time. "She had a real motherly character, and loved me truly from her heart," remembers Jagdishji.

About his training Jagdishji says that the *Ustad* has not perhaps said so much about the *shehnai*, and its music to anyone else as much as he has imparted to his dear disciple Jagdish. During the days of his training Khan Sahib would instruct his student to be awake till he came to teach him. The obedient student would remain awake till late in the night when everybody would retire to bed after the day's work. The *Ustad* would come and call the disciple, "Jagdish, you are not asleep?" "No *Ustad*", the patient young disciple would unfailingly answer. "O.K., then I am going upstairs, and would play a tune from there. You will have to listen to it carefully, and then repeat it from down-stairs. Will you?" the master would probe the heart of his disciple, as the eager disciple would reply positively. Thus, the strenuous training session would go on. Jagdishji would try to repeat the tunes that his *Ustad* would play from up-stairs, but most of the times he would fail to follow his teacher flawlessly. Still the *Ustad* would be happy with the disciple because what he wanted was not the immaculate reproduction of the tunes, it was the devotion, the earnestness of the student to make himself suitable for the rigorous training. Jagdishji reveals that those who would not obey Ustad Bismillah Khan are not liked by him. He wants to see true devotion and love for work in the human character. He detests impatience in place of desire for through learning, and the covetouness for glamour, money and fame in the modern generation. "One can never become a master with such drawbacks of character!" He declares, "Only true devotion, only unfailing perseverence can make you a pure and real musician. Otherwise, you will be an artist, but there will be no divine union, no *"assar"* in your music." The master is totally correct, and that is the reason why we don't see another Bismillah Khan rising in the sky of classical music to day.

Jagdish describes his *Ustad* as a simple and unpretentious person. He loves to eat simple food-preparations with lamb and green vegetables, *chutney*, sliced onions, *roti* with pats of pure *ghee* over it. Potato with *badi*, and onion with *badi* are among his favourite dishes. He loves green vegetables such as *parmal*, *turai* and *tinda*. He is not a fastidious person about his daily food. Beef is forbidden in the house of Ustad Bismillah Khan. A strange truth, which makes one more curious about the open and yet mysterious life of Khan Sahib. Similar as his food-habit, Khan Sahib is not fussy about his clothes. He wears plain *kurtas* and *pyjamas*, normally white in colour. During programmes and other special occasions he would wear a *sherwani* (a long coat) over tight *pyjamas*. He is not particular about the fabric of the clothes too. Any good material like *malmal* or silk would suit him perfectly.

There is no conflict of religion in the house-hold of the *shehnai*-maestro. His most favourite disciple Jagdish belongs to a Hindu family, who learnt music while staying at his house. The *Ustad* unfailingly sends money to each member of his party during each festival of the year, and there is no discrimination between Hindu or Muslim or anyone belonging to any other religion. The harmony is not just in his music, Khan Sahib has complete concord in his character too. No discrepancies, no blots are to be found anywhere in his music or life. Till recently, Vishnu Prasanna and Mohanlal, who belong to the family of the famous *shehnai*-player Nandlal, were members of Khan Sahib's party.

Jagdishji's daughter, Bageshwari, who is the first, and the only one woman *shehnai*-player in the whole world has also learnt from Ustad Bismillah Khan. She went to him in 1989, as Jagdishji himself says. She is still learning from Khan Sahib. Khan Sahib talks about her very fondly. One wonders, thinking about his conservative background, where women are supposed to stay behind the curtains. But the *Ustad*, being a true artist, knows no difference between a man and a woman. Anyone who works hard, and is sincere earns his blessed favour.

A GENUINE AND LOYAL FRIEND

As a friend and colleague Ustad Bismillah Khan is a most unusual personality-simple, honest, out spoken, and yet extremely loyal. He takes one of his friends practically, to all his foreign tours.

He did not forget to write to his friend, Abdul Haq, while going through the important tour of the U.S.A. A friend who gave him hospitality during his not so famous days, remained dear, as before to him even when he became eminent and known to the whole world. His concern about his friend's and colleague's wellbeing surpasses all the boundaries of the shallow social norms. I experienced this truth once, during a function.

The venue was Siri Fort Auditorium of Delhi, the ocassion was the 70th birthday celebration of the grand sitar-maestro Pt. Ravi Shankar. Because of my childhood association with him, I call Panditji, Robuda. In every important work of my life, Robuda has lent me his support going out of his way. He has written hundreds of letters of recommendations for various projects that I undertook, like celebrating the birth-anniversary of my teacher Begum Akhtar in a five-day-festival, and plunging myself into a monumental task of working on the professional-singing women of our country. It is always Robuda, who gives a pat on my back. Naturally, I was there at the auditorium, sitting right at the front with him on that great evening. The auspicious light was lit by Robuda's eight-year old daughter, while he gleamed happily with his newly wedded wife. Robuda was invited on the dais along with

Ustad Bismillah Khan and the well-known painter Satish Gujral. Khan Sahib was to garland and welcome Panditji, while Satish Gujral presented a painting on the theme 'the spirit of freedom' to him. Khan Sahib garlanded Pt. Ravi Shankar, and series of speeches on Panditji followed. At the end, as the chief guest, Khan Sahib was invited to give his speech. He came on to the mike beaming candidly like a ten-year old boy, and said a few words of praise for Panditji. He prayed for his long life and made a *dua*. In a split second then his eyes glittered with a naughty, mischievous smile. He said, "I am older than Ravi Shankar in age, as well as an admirer of his music. Only one request I have to make-*aab aur woh shadi na kare*. (He should not marry any more). While present in the hall I was not only embarrassed, but was angry with Khan Sahib as he said these words to Panditji. So much so that the *Puria Dhaneshri* that he played that evening, followed by a *dhun* became jarring is my ears. Was he out of tune that evening? May be I was out of tune with the grandmaster, and did not understand his frank and innocent style of speech!

This time, as I visited Benaras to know him, his family, his ambience, we were sitting in the large covered verandah of his courtyard after a gruelling session of photography and interviews, Khan Sahib compelled me to sing for him. With closed eyes he listened to my *Bhairavi*. At the end of my music came boiled eggs, tea and sweets as *nashta* (a light meal). With great affection Khan Sahib patted on my head. Looking straight into my eyes, he said, "I know that you too have fallen in love, with *sur* and have started conversing with the Higher worlds through your music. Do not disclose anything to anyone. Wah! This is Benaras, this is Benarasi music, this is the Banaras *ang*." He gave a hearty laughter. A laughter befitting of a saint or a *Pir*, a *fakir*. Searching his guileless face with my astonished eyes, I could understand then the meanings of the words, he spoke to Pandit Ravi Shankar the other day in the Siri Fort Auditorium. I remembered the bright smile on the face of Panditji. The admiring way with which he accepted Khan Sahib's comments. A little knot that I had in my mind for Khan Sahib was totally washed away. I realized, how difficult for a human, living in a modern society today to give and take an honest opinion. I admired Robuda for his tolerance and respected Khan Sahib for his artless courage, with which he could express his opinion to his colleague.

The Indian Council for Cultural Relations organises exchange programmes of various musicians with the countries abroad. The council is responsible for sending the artists to the foreign countries. Ustad Bismillah Khan and his party was to be sent to Iran, in October, 1993. I knew that Khan Sahib was in Delhi, and I would have an opportunity to take his interview. It was necessary for starting with the book on him that I was planning to write. Fortunately, I rang up ICCR, in order to know about Khan Sahib's where, abouts, otherwise I would have gone to Rajdhani Hotel in search of him, where he stayed when I met him in Naina Devis's house with Ammi (My teacher, Begum Akhtar). Khan Sahib loves to stay in that hotel. I was told as I rang up ICCR that Ustad Bismillah Khan and his party was staying in Lodhi Hotel. I first knocked the room no. 203. Khan Sahib's grand-son, Bande Ali opened the door. He told me that Khan Sahib would give me exactly one hour for the interview. I was accompanied by my dear friend Avinash Pasricha, the photo-editor of the Span magazine. Avinash has been a companion and close friend since the days when I worked on the professional-singing women. We have been together while seeking and examining many difficult artists. We invariably exchange our glances before knocking at the doors whenever we expect trouble. We went on knocking for sometime on the door of the room where Khan Sahib was staying, but no reply came. Somebody passing through the corridor said, "*Khan Sahib aajkal uncha sunte hai* (These days Khan Sahib can not hear unless one speaks loudly), you will have to speak loudly." I looked at my friend Avinash. He is also a little deaf. A grand master of his own work is hard of hearing! These are the strange ways of life. Those who can hear the music of the supreme worlds, perhaps slowly shut their ears to the mundane world of discord. So they say about Beethoven, the great German composer, who became deaf and was cut off from the world, as he composed some of the best pieces of his musical work. Homer was blind, but he was a seer. I know of Sitara Devi, who suffers from acute arthritis, yet almost for 70 years now, she has been steady in her dancing career. She broke all the records, dancing for 9 hours continuouly. Finally, the door was opened by an elderly gentleman. I came to know later that he is the only friend of Khan Sahib. I saw Khan Sahib coming out of the bath wrapped in a big hotel towel. His legs were covered with a pair of socks till his knees, and he was wearing a vest on the upper part of his body. He was totally oblivious of his appearance before me and my friend Avinash. Avinash's assistant started arranging the lights and the flash-umbrella. Khan Sahib sat on his bed. He didn't change, and without any fuss faced the camera in the manner that he was. I went near and touched his feet. He looked carefully at me and said, "*Are ye to hamari banaras ki ladki hai* (She belongs to Benaras)!" He turned towards his friend and said, "*Are Siddheshwari Ki Shagird hai* (She is the student of Siddheshwari Devi)." The friend intrigued said, "But just now you have said that she is the disciple of Begum Akhtar?" Khan Sahib chuckled, "That is the fun. She has learnt from two great masters who were enemies to each other. But over the phone they said that you were Ganguly? That is why I demanded a lakh rupees before giving an interview. Why did you not tell me that it was you?" What he said was true. Khan Sahib really demanded one lakh rupees to give an interview. I rang up Benaras through STD and was shocked and hurt to know his strange demand. Presently Khan

Sahib said, "Ganguly is what? Is it a Hindu name? I thought you were a Muslim. I do not forget anything. In fact, I remember those were the days of *Ramazaan*, and around 7 o'clock you gave your teacher *Iftari* and she said, *"Tum bhi kha lo* (You too eat) because you were also keeping *rozaa*. Are Allah, how devoted musicians are to their teachers!" I bent my head down and touching his feet said, *"Khan Sahib, ek lakh rupia main Khan se laaun? Main to ghabda gai thi. Khidmat ke liye sar hazir hai* (Khan Sahib, where from shall I bring a lakh rupees. I became so nervous and a enxious. My head is available to be sacrifieced in your service)." His eyes became wet and he said, "Look at her! I have earned crores with those words of yours. I have received my fees."

Avinash presented him with a broad envelop. He thought Khan Sahib would be happy because there were photographs of Khan Sahib's young days in it. With collyrium in his eyes, robust with black and curly hair, Khan Sahib smiled in those photographs. He did not put a second glance at the photographs. Just went through them casually.

He is least interested to see how he looked in his youth. He is the only man I have come across whose past does not haunt him. He was not bothered about the yesteryears, although his friend went through the photographs with great interest.

Khan Sahib in a matter of fact manner reminded me that he had only one hour to spare. He had lot of formalities to go through with visa etc. I told him that I had cooked some *korma*, *roti* and some *kheer* (the Bengali preparation with a special jaggery) for him, as I said I began asking him questions. I went prepared with hundred questions. Avinash started clicking his camera. I quickly got up and covered Khan Sahib's feet with a shawl. He laughed saying, "Don't worry. I am what I am. Nothing to cover. Nothing to camouflage. Nothing is there in my life which I can not relate without keeping my head high. Thanks to Allah!"

He started answering the questions in a very dry and curt manner, since the initial questions were the usual ones which Khan Sahib had been answering for the past 49 years. One could see the typical Western professionalism as he talked. There was nothing inspiring, nothing extraordinary in his manners. Everything was plain and customary in his bearing. He kept on looking at his watch. As the session continued, he reminded me that it was already two hours. I quickly got his food heated up in the kitchen of the hotel through a bearer and served him. I told him it was late, he should have his lunch and rest.

We were not yet half way through, and Khan Sahib said, "I am sorry. I have absolutely no time for another few months to come. I will have to go here and there. No time even to breathe." He took a morsel of *korma* and *roti*. His face lit up. With his eyes gleaming with the typical naughtiness of a little boy he enquired. "*Tumne pakaya* (Have you, yourself cooked it)?" I promptly answered his query with a counter question, "Who is the most beautiful woman that you have admired?" Looking at me from the corner of his eyes he said, "You are naughty. I would better not answer." It was a different Khan Sahib.

Just a bite of aesthetic food had changed his demeanour. He related a series of unforgettable moments of his life. I asked him if he was fond of cooking, since I could become Begum Akhtar's *shagird* as I was a good cook. He gave his familiar, hearty laugh and said that Begum Akhtar was an exquisite woman. He also said that indeed all good musicians are fond of good eating. As they have to stay away from home for long periods of time, they would cook their own food. Like a typical housewife he described me that the secret of preparing meat was mixing everything, and then putting the whole thing in a slow fire. While doing the *riaz* the musician would stir the preparation occasionally until the meat became tender. The trick was, 200 and 50 gms of mustard oil was to be brought in boiling temperature, 10 gms of cloves was to be seasoned in that oil, and the meat would be ready.

Khan Sahib told me that unless the musicians would know how to cook, they would not survive during their tours. May be it is true. Just the other day, a friend of mine, married in the legendary Pahari Sanyal family was describing how Ali Akbar Khan Sahib is fond of cooking while he stays in the U.S.A. I remember, on my every birthday, no matter wherever my teacher Begum Akhtar would be, she would come to my place to cook mutton-stew with *khari* masala (chopped, not ground spices) for me. I recollected the memory of Hirabai Barodekar, who would visit my maternal uncle Shree S.K. Bose, and cook *biriyani.* The taste of her delectable *biriyani,* I have not forgot till date. While I was lost in these thoughts Khan Sahib asked for another helping of the *korma* which I had brought for him. He started telling me of the past, of the Princely estate of Dumraon, where his father and grandfather served as court-musicians. The regular gifts from the Maharaj to their house came not in kilos but in quintals. There was no dearth of anything. Fruits, jaggery, pure *ghee,* special quality of rice and flour, fish, meat and vegetables arrived in huge quantities. There was no need for any money or salary. I asked Khan Sahib if he thought that his sons would be able to establish themselves as individual artists. His reply was, they would if they really persevere, if they understand that music is like meditation, and there is no short-cut, to success. He told that he could prepare the food for someone, and put it before him. But the other person would have to use hands to pick up the food, to deposit it inside the mouth, he then would have to chew the food, digest, and ultimately assimilate it in his system. All these could not be done by the person who cooks the food and serves it. He said, "I can take my sons to the concerts with me. Give them the opportunity to be on the stage with me, but then they must be worthy enough to be spotted by the organizers as individual artists, as I was once spotted! Their work must be solid enough, and powerful that they will be invited alone in the programmes. I can not do it for them! They themselves must endeavour for it. One has to come out of the shade of the other person in order to find out fresh dimension for oneself! And for that you need true work and devotion. Nothing can be achieved without hard work and dedication." After a few thoughtful moments he said again, "Now, look at you, yourself. You have learnt from two celebrated *Ustad,* whose music not only I admired but they had inspired me also with their music directly or indirectly. But you have your own aroma. I enjoyed listening to you without being reminded of your famous teachers. That is individuality which comes from true work and devotion. If you had been just a copy of Siddheshwari Devi or Begum Akhtar, the listener will feel nostalgic, but will fail to know you as a separate and singular musician. Similarly, I can give my sons chances of facing an audience, but if they won't prepare themselves by understanding the *ragas, bandishes* and with practice, how will they be able to strengthen themselves to face the crowd alone? No one will do it on their behalf. You must yourself search for and find the place that is existing for yourself. There is no other way, nor any other rule." I knew that Khan Sahib was correct. One has to find the path for himself or herself. Others can show you the direction, but can not walk or work for you. And you remain behind if you refuse to walk your destined path. One may go on complaining about lack of opportunities, about all sorts of things, but the real problem lies hidden in yourself, and only in yourself. If you do not work, the fruit of the work is not for you, and if you work half-heartedly no body is satisfied with your work. This is true forever and ever.

He told me that the secret of life's success was in *'Iman'*, the righteousness of a person. Whatever happens one should not give up honesty, and be led by conscience. His disciple Jagdish entered with his daughter Bageshwari, as he was telling all these things to me. He fondly introduced me to his disciple and his daughter. Bageshwari is learning from Khan Sahib. The *Ustad* very proudly stated that she was the first and only woman in the world to learn and play the *shehnai*. Jagdishji wanted to invite us to his house for meal since I was allergic to the alien food of the hotels, but I refused. I was very busy, and did not want to waste a couple of hours eating. Khan Sahib surprised at my refusal exclaimed, "And see there you come with cooked food, and what good food you bring for us. This is called Iman. May Allah take care of you." He blessed me with the same words with which he had blessed his disciple Jagdish just a few minutes before as he entered the room. His benevolence touched me with a feel of tenderness in the heart. Jagdishji served himself with the food in the same plate in which his *Ustad* had eaten. Khan Sahib patted him. I remembered my teacher Siddheshwari Devi, who often used to say, "You are born from my soul. You are like a little *farishta* (Angel) to me. I can easily sacrifice my two daughters Shanta and Savita since they are the outcome of my desire. You are the fruit of my *Sadhna*, and you are more dear to me." Really, a true *Ustad* does not care if the *shagird*, the student is his or her own son or daughter or someone else who belongs to a different religion, family or community. The bondage between the teacher and the student is beyond all words and descriptions.

As I mused a while moved by Khan Sahib's words, I heard a terrible uproar outside. The slogans were bring raised by the campaigners for the Delhi elections. Funny, distorted and prerecorded songs of eminent singers were booming in the air, coming out of the microphones, carried in scooters. A horrendous sound pounded on the ear-drums, which I later found out was supposed to be the conch and *Khartal* campaigning for a lotus or a hand with a *'choli ke peechhe kya hai'* song. Everything was sickeningly non-musical. The microphone was announcing about the great leaders who were supposed to visit the area. Watching at Khan Sahib's expressions, I felt embarrassed, and responsible for Delhi, my town. Avinash requested if he could come out of the hotel room, so that he could take a few photographs in a different back-ground. Khan Sahib closed his eyes, made face, blocked his ears, and said, "*Tauba*. Allah help me. This is the level of our Indian politics. They are announcing about the arrival of the leaders in your area. Once elected for five years, you don't see their faces again. This politics has ruined our country. If there is anything that makes this world not worth living, it is here in these slogans, full of wicked lies. Is it this freedom that we dreamt of on the auspicious day of 15th August in 1947, when I played *shehnai* to give the nation the message of our independence? Are we only to get these vile treacheries in the name of independence?" I was unable to answer him. In fact, I did not know what to say. A little while after I asked Khan Sahib when I could come to Benaras to visit him, and take the rest of the interview. He smiled and answered, "Don't worry. I will come back. Otherwise what will happen to the hundred people, I look after?" He must truly be a worried man, I knew. I thought of the days which his disciple Jagdishji had described when Khan Sahib would give the money for the whole month to his disciple and ask him to run the house. No Jagdish could have been able to manage such a big family that Khan Sahib now has, with economy. I understood the cause of his irritation, his curt and brusque manners. How could a man with such a great burden over his back be in a happy mood? He must be a very anxious man.

As Jagdishji met me after the interviews were complete, he said that Khan Sahib was not happy with his own behaviour after I left the hotel on the day when I took the first interview. He regrettingly said to Jagdishji, "She was a very nice person. I should have been more considerate to her. It was not good of me to be so blunt." I was happy to hear this. I was a little disheartened that day, but I liked the frankness of Khan Sahib's nature. It was easy to forget the harshness as one noticed that whatever he said was true. Nothing was exaggerated, nothing was hidden. He spoke in a plain and indifferent language which suits his whole character. History will never repeat a character like Ustad Bismillah Khan again vis-a-vis the whole galaxy of musicians, including my own teachers. There are no side-lanes or by-lanes in his life. No juicy anecdotes to be hidden from anyone. He is an open book, which anyone can read and get amazed knowing of the awesome love that he has for his music. He is lonely without his music. He has visited our sorrowful world as a freak of nature to solace our hearts with the gift of his soulful music. No one like him among the *shehnai*-players was before, no one will be after him. He is one and unique. The coming generation should at least have a glimpse of the era that was fortunate enough to receive the blessings of Ustad Bismillah Khan's music. Only when one walks the path of the religion of music, one become able to know that Allah and Bramhan are one.

Appendix

Appendix

GENEOLOGY

GENERATION OF USTAD BISMILLAH KHAN

RESIDENCE DUMRAON (BIHAR)

SALAAR HUSAIN KHAN

SOHRAB HUSAIN KHAN

HUSAIN BUX KHAN

RASOOL BUX KHAN

PAIGAMBER BUX KHAN

- SHAMSUDDIN KHAN
  Alias (SHAMSUL)
  (Elder Brother)
- KAMRUDDIN KHAN
  Alias (BISMILLAH KHAN)
  - MEHTAB HUSAIN
    - MOHD. HASNAIN
      MOHD. SIBTE HASAN
      RAZEE HASAN
      (One daughter)
  - NAYYAR HUSAIN
    - NASIR HUSAIN
      YAVAR HUSAIN
      ASAD
      FARHAT
      (4 daughters)
  - ZAMIN HUSAIN
    - JAVED
    - GUDDU
      BABU
      AFAQUE
      (5 daughters)
  - KAZIM HUSAIN
    - NAZRE HAṢAN
      PARVEZ
  - NAZIM HUSAIN
    (Unmarried)

SHAMSUDDIN KHAN (ELDER BROTHER)

- ABRAR HUSAIN
  - FAIZ ALI
  - HADI HUSAIN
  - 3 daughters
- ALI HAIDER
  - HADI HUSAIN
  - 3 daughters
- ALI AKBER
  - BANDE ALI
  - 3 daughters
- ALI ABBAS
  - RAZA ABBAS
  - 2 daughters
- ABUL HASAN
  - No Issue
- KALBE HASAN
  - Unmarried

MATERNAL RELATION (VARANASI)

- RAMZAN ALI (PER NANA)
  - RAJATS ALI (NANA)
    - VILAYAT ALI
      - 3 daughters
    - SADIQUE ALI
      - 3 daughters (One married to elder brother Shamsuddin Khanand another to Bismillah Khan)
    - ALI BUX (Ustad of Bismillah Khan)
      - 3 daughters

LIST OF RECORDS

ACC NO. 13
RAGAS : BHIMPALASI
TILAK KAMOD
JOGIA
KAJRI
POORVI
CHAITI

ACC NO. 437
RAGAS : MULTANI: TEEN TAAL, DHUN
GHAZAL PAHADI DHUN
BEHAG: TEEN TAAL
DHUN

ACC No. 740
RAGAS : RAGESHWARI
SHIVARANJANI

ACC NO. 749
RAGAS : RAGESHWARI
SHIVARANJANI

ACC NO. 788
RAGAS : BHIMPALASI, KAJRI, CHAITI
TILAK KAMOD
MISHRA KHAMAJ, BASANT BAHAR
MARU BEHAG
CHANDRAKAUNS, DHUN (BHANGRA)

ACC NO. 789
RAGAS : SHUDH KALYAN, DADRA, DHUN,
YAMAN, POORVI

DHUN (GHAZAL BHAIRAVI)
SHANTA PRASAD, BISMILLAH KHAN
& VILAYAT KHAN

ACC NO. 5244
RAGAS : LALIT
SARANG

ACC NO. 8929
RAGAS : BAHAR
MISHRA KHAMAJ

ACC NO. 6726
RAGAS : DHUN, BHUPALI TODI, JHAPTAL,
BAGESHWARI

ACC NO. 7156
RAGAS : TODI
MISHRA THUMRI

ACC NO. 4002
RAGAS : KOMAL RISHABH ASAWARI
SHUDH SARANG
HANZ KINKINI

ACC NO. 9221
RAGAS : BAIRAGI BHAIRAVI, GHAZAL EASD 1373
SHYAM KALYAN: TEEN TAAL
BHANGRA

ACC NO. 9173
RAGAS : LALIT: TEEN TAAL
DHUN
MULTANI
DHUN GHAZAL

ACC NO. 3377
RAGAS : GUJRI TODI
SHANKARA

ACC NO. 3653
RAGAS : BASANT
POORVI DHUN

ACC NO. 5485
RAGAS : YAMAN
BRINDABANI SARANG

ACC NO. 8504
RAGAS : KAJRI, POORVI, CHAITI
TILAK KAMOD

ACC NO. 5319
RAGAS : BEHAG
KALAVALI

ACC NO. 5486
RAGAS : YAMAN
BRINDABANI SARANG

ACC NO. 9232
RAGAS : MADAMAT SARANG
BHAIRAVI, DHUN, RAM DHUN

ACC NO. 9105
RAGAS : JAUNPURI
IMAN KALYAN, POORVI DHUN
EMI-EC S D - 2797

ACC NO. 2968
RAGAS : BAGESHWARI
SAHANA

ACC NO. 6787
RAGAS : GUNKALI
SHUDH KALYAN, PAHADI DHUN

ACC NO. 8081
RAGAS : AHIR BHAIRAVI
BHIMPALASI

ACC NO. 2332
RAGAS : BASANT
SURMALHAR
BHIMPALASI
POORVI DHUN
KADAR CHAITI

ACC NO. 2375
RAGAS : KHAMAJ
DUEI

ACC NO. 2358
RAGAS : MALKAUNS
DHUN
RAGHUPATI RAGHAVA 1966
E-A 1306
EMI HMV

ACC NO. 3146
RAGAS : YAMAN
BHAIRAVI THUMRI

ACC NO. 8912
RAGAS : SHYAM KALAYAN: TEEN TAAL
DURGA: TEEN TAAL

ACC NO. 6184
RAGAS : SARANG
CHANDRAKAUNS

ACC NO. 8970
RAGAS : MALKAUNS
DESH
THUMRI TILAK KAMOD

ACC NO. 6892
RAGAS : BEHAG: TEEN TAAL
KALAWATI: TEEN TAAL

ACC NO. 9180
RAGAS : SARANG
CHANDRAKAUNS

ACC NO. 8960
RAGAS : BILAS KHANI TODI: TEEN TAAL
BAGESHWARI: TEEN TAAL
DHUN: DADRA

ACC NO. 2369
RAGAS : BILAWAL
CHANDRAKAUNS

ACC NO. 3009
RAGAS : BHAIRAVI
MULTANI PILOO THUMRI

ACC NO. 2389
RAGAS : POORIA DHANASHRI
BHAIRAVI

ACC NO. 5319
RAGAS : BEHAG: TEEN TAAL
KALAWATI: TEEN TAL

GLOSSARY

Rasa	-	Aesthetic expression involving particular emotions
Subzi	-	A vegetable preparation
Karela	-	Bitter-gourd
Chutney	-	A preparation made by grinding fresh uncooked vegetables like coriander leaves, raw mangoes, mint etc.
Vyanjan	-	A dish
Patra	-	Character of a play, also a vessel
Rasaswadan	-	The enjoyment of taste
Sur	-	Musical notes
Layakavi	-	Musical harmoniousness
Sadharnikaran	-	Making things ordinary
Aloukik	-	Sublime
Ouchitya	-	Proper, correct
Guru-Shishya Parampara	-	Traditional relationship between the master and disciple
Bindis	-	Decorative dots used on the forehead
Panchadhatu	-	A mixture of copper, iron, gold, silver, brass
Divas	-	Oil lamps
Jalebi	-	An Indian sweet
Parantha	-	Kneaded flour is shaped and cooked in clarified butter
Laddoos	-	Indian sweets associated with auspicious occasions
Jhumka	-	Ear ornament

Mujra	-	Dance and musical performance by professional women trained in the arts. Over the years this has become almost synonymous with prostitution and hence derogatory
Gajra	-	Garland of flowers meant for the hair
Panwala	-	The man who sells beetle leaves
Kunj	-	A garden
Pathashala	-	A school of learning
Yajnas	-	Sacrificial rituals involving fire worship
Sa	-	The first musical note on the octave
Mamu	-	Maternal uncle
Chotte Mamu	-	Younger maternal uncle
Sandhyarat	-	The ritual worship performed at sunset, with the sounding of bells and shells
Tats	-	Jute mats
Ganda	-	A ceremonial thread tied on the wrist of a disciple by a guru
Assar	-	The essence
Tanga	-	Horse drawn carriage
Riaz	-	Practice
Kotha	-	A place of residence and performance of professional singing women
Nayika	-	Heroine
Ched Chaad	-	Teasing
Dua	-	Obeisance
Gunah	-	Sin
Bandishes	-	Compositions
Alap	-	A prelude to a *raga*

Dangal - Duel

Ghats - River banks

Saraswati - The goddess of learning and music

Ilm - Talent

Juggalbandi - Pairing up

Index